Southern Publishin ... ee

MAKE IT PLAIN

THE PLAN OF SALVATION MADE SIMPLE

PAUL HEUBACH

This book was
Edited by Don Short
Designed by Mark O'Connor

Type set: 10/11 Palatino

Printed in U.S.A.

Library of Congress Cataloging in Publication Data

Heubach, Paul C
Make it plain.
1. Christian life—Seventh-day Adventist authors.
I. Title.
BV4501.2.H388 248.4'8673 80-13864
ISBN 0-8127-0295-6

ISBN 0-8127-0295-6

Bible Quotations

All references to the Bible not otherwise designated are taken from the King James Version. Other versions quoted, with the abbreviations used, are as follows:

Amplified—The Amplified Bible and New Testament. By permission of The Lockman Foundation.

Berkeley—THE MODERN LANGUAGE BIBLE, The Berkeley Version, Copyright 1945, 1959, 1969 by Zondervan Publishing House, and is used by permission.

Moffatt—The Bible: A New Translation, by James Moffatt. Copyright, 1954. Reprinted by permission of Harper and Row, Publishers, Inc.

NEB—The New English Bible. Copyright, The Delegates of the Oxford University Press and The Syndics of the Cambridge University Press, 1961, 1970. Reprinted by permission.

NIV—The New International Version. Copyright 1973, 1978 by The New York Bible Society International and is used by permission.

Phillips—The New Testament in Modern English. Copyright, J. B. Phillips, 1958. Used by permission of The Macmillan Company.

RSV—Revised Standard Version.

TEV—The Bible in Today's English Version. Copyright, American Bible Society, 1976.

Dedicated to those who sincerely desire to be Christians but find the way difficult and often confusing.

CONTENTS

Preface

"Please, Pastor, Make It Plain!"

Answering the telephone one evening, I recognized the voice of a friend who lived up in the High Sierra mountains. After a few words of greeting, she said that they had recently had a series of sermons in their church on righteousness by faith, and the speaker had made the subject so complicated that everyone was thoroughly confused. She then asked if I would come up for the weekend and talk about the subject and answer some of their questions. She concluded by saying, "And please, Paul, make it plain and simple so that we mountain folk can understand it."

At times theologians have made the simple truths of the gospel so complicated that many have had difficulty in grasping their true meaning. While the great truths of Christianity are profound, the heart of the gospel should be made so plain that a child can understand it. Didn't Jesus say, "Let the little children come unto Me"? And didn't He tell Peter to feed His "lambs"?

To the man on the street, much of Christianity is a foreign language. Christians have a vocabulary all their own. They use terms that are understood only by those within the group.

You may hear a conversation between a Seventh-day Adventist Christian and someone else go something like this:

"I've been in the truth about ten years now."

"What's that you were in?"

"Oh, I accepted the message some ten years ago."

"The message? What message?"

"The third angel's message."

"Why the third? What happened to the other two?"

The problem of semantics is always present in communication on any subject, but especially is this true in the field of religion.

To a person who has never been to church, who knows nothing about the Bible, and who may never have been around religious people, the simplest truths understood by all who are Christians would not be too meaningful. "There is power in the blood." "Washed in the blood of the Lamb." "Are you saved?" "Have you been born again?" "Let Jesus come into your heart." All these expressions sound very strange to the uninitiated. And this is not to mention such terms as "justification," "sanctification," "glorification," "imputed and imparted righteousness," "the atonement," and even "the gospel of the kingdom."

The word *gospel* means "good news." To many people, I know the gospel is not good news. Take such statements as these: "You are a sinner, and 'the wages of sin is death.' " " 'The hour of his judgment is come,' 'and who shall be able to stand?' " "Without holiness 'no man shall see the Lord.' " " 'Be ye therefore perfect, even as your Father which is in heaven is perfect.' " From some points of view, these statements are not good news. More than one person has been led to say, in thought if not in words, "I wish I had never heard it. If I didn't know about it, I wouldn't have to change my life. But now that I have heard it, I am obligated to live it. So here goes, I don't want to burn."

What a pity! Jesus said, "These things have I spoken unto you, that my joy might remain in you, and that your joy might be full" (John 15:11). He also said, "Peace I leave with you, my peace I give unto you" (John 14:27). These words cannot be true in our experience unless we understand His message in terms of real good news.

In this book I propose to make plain the "good news" in terms that can be understood. I shall endeavor to present the great truths of the Bible in terms of life where people live it, and hope that these truths will be seen as the joyful news the word *gospel* implies.

I am indebted to a great many for insights that have warmed my heart through the years and that will appear on these pages. Most of these people have enriched my life in ways that cannot be put in words. My colleagues and friends have contributed more than I realize, I am sure, and if any idea expressed in this book is helpful, these all should be thanked.

Chapter 1

A Personal Experience

"Come on up, Paul. If you can make it, we'll have a good time." The theme for a Week of Prayer in a Christian academy was "Steps to Christ." I could see Jesus at the top of the stairs, and His call was made very appealing by the speaker. I decided to take the steps. All too soon I discovered that I wasn't very successful. I would stumble and fall into some of my old habits. Sometimes when I thought I was taking a real step toward the goal, I would fall back two. It seemed impossible to reach the Good Master and to live up to His standards.

I discussed the matter with a minister, and he told me that I was trying too hard. "Just let go, and let God," he said. "Reach up with the hand of faith and grasp the hand of God, and He will see you through." Well, I tried letting go and trusting God, but God didn't seem to do anything. I would reach up and try to grasp the hand of God, but there was nothing tangible there. "Just surrender," the minister said, but I couldn't understand that.

Another minister came along and preached a sermon on fighting "the good fight of faith." He compared the Christian life to a battle and a march. " 'Endure hardness, as a good soldier of Jesus Christ,' " he said, and we sang "Onward Christian Soldiers" with enthusiasm. That sounds more like it, I thought, and I determined to battle it through. I made some new resolutions and started up the steps again. But I was no more successful at this than I had been in the first place.

The more I thought about it, the more puzzling this whole business of living the Christian life became. One minister says, "Surrender." The next one says, "Fight like everything." How can a person do both?

"The trouble with you, Paul," still another minister told me, "is that you have never been converted. Once you have been born again, it will be altogether different." He explained that conversion was not just an improvement of the old nature, but a new life altogether—a complete transformation. He compared conversion to the change that takes place between a caterpillar and a butterfly. A butterfly is not just an improved caterpillar. It is an entirely new creature. "Now, what would you think of a butterfly who all the time wished he could crawl around in the dust with the caterpillars? That would be absurd, wouldn't it?"

The more I thought about that, the more confused I became. "There are some things about the caterpillar life that still appeal to me. I guess I'm not a butterfly yet," I thought.

Another of his illustrations involved a wolf and a lamb. Conversion is a transformation of character such as would take place if God changed a wolf into a lamb. The lamb would be a new creature, and not just a wolf in sheep's clothing. "What would you think of a lamb who was found drooling over a dead carcass?" he asked. That, too, had some interesting implications for me. After hearing him, I was sure I had never been converted.

It was made plain to me that Jesus wanted men with pure thoughts, a clean heart, and a sinless life. "As a man 'thinketh in his heart, so is he' " (Proverbs 23:7). According to John, "whosoever hateth his brother is a murderer" (1 John 3:15). Jesus said, "Whosoever looketh on a woman to lust after her hath committed adultery with her already in his heart" (Matthew 5:28). If to think an evil thought is as bad as to do an evil deed, one might as well go ahead and do it. He will burn anyway. Is this true?

What if I should deny myself all the pleasures of this world and then not make it to the world to come? I will have missed both. Maybe I ought to have all the fun I can now and take my chances on the hereafter. Can I be sure of life eternal? It seems at times that the prerequisites are too high. We can never measure up anyway, so why try?

The Bible talks about "holiness, without which no man shall see the Lord" (Hebrews 12:14). It says, "Be ye holy; for I am holy" (1 Peter 1:16). "Be ye therefore perfect, even as your Father which is in heaven is perfect" (Matthew 5:48). How can I ever be either holy or perfect?

Then, too, there is coming a day of judgment. Every sin I have ever committed has been recorded. Every evil thought and every idle word will be included. One unconfessed sin on the record book will keep me out of the kingdom of heaven. Is this correct? What if I have forgotten one?

These are some of the thoughts and questions that went through my mind in my younger years, some of the experiences I had in trying to live the Christian life. I wrestled with some of these problems for years.

I was brought up in a Christian home and early learned to pray and to sing hymns and gospel songs.

My mother was a sincere Lutheran Christian, but because there was no Lutheran church in Winnemucca, Nevada, where I was born, I attended a Methodist Sunday School. In order to be brought up right, and to make certain that I was properly indoctrinated, however, my mother had me study Luther's catechism at home. I'm sure I didn't get everything straight, for I came to understand erroneously that Jesus loved only "good" boys and that some day when I died I would go to heaven. It was also registered in my mind that Jesus didn't love bad boys and that some day if they didn't change, they would go to hell, where they would burn forever and ever. When I became a Seventh-day Adventist my perspective on many of the theological issues changed, but then I faced other perplexing problems as indicated above.

As I grew older and life became more and more complicated the prerequisites to citizenship in heaven became more and more difficult. I found within me growing desires that seemed to be in conflict with the requirements of God, and meeting these requirements became increasingly impossible. Other questions arose in my mind, but fortunately I had wonderful parents and later a host of friends and teachers who had wrestled with the same problems and who helped to establish my faith.

I think of the experience of the two boys in Sam Walter Foss's poem:

> A boy was born 'mid little things,
> Between a little world and sky—
> And dreamed not of the cosmic rings
> Round which the circling planets fly.
>
> He lived in little works and thoughts,

Where little ventures grow and plod,
And paced and ploughed his little plots,
And prayed unto his little God.

But as the mighty system grew,
His faith grew faint with many scars;
The Cosmos widened in his view—
But God was lost among His stars.

Another boy in lowly days,
As he, to little things was born,
But gathered lore in woodland ways,
And from the glory of the morn.

As wider skies broke on his view,
God greatened in his growing mind;
Each year he dreamed his God anew,
And left the older God behind.

He saw the boundless scheme dilate,
In star and blossom, sky and clod;
And as the universe grew great,
He dreamed for it a greater God.

In the pages that follow, I hope to share with you some basic concepts that have helped me, with the hope that you may be encouraged by them.

Chapter 2

I Love Life

I am come that they might have life, and that they might have it more abundantly (John 10:10).

He that hath the Son hath life; and he that hath not the Son of God hath not life (1 John 5:12).

What would it take to enable you to say, "Ah, this is the life?" What, to you, is really living? Have you ever heard anyone say, "I don't want to be a Christian yet; I want to live a little first"? What do you suppose is meant?

Jesus said, "I am come that they might have life, and that they might have it more abundantly" (John 10:10). He did not say, "I am come that they might have a new set of rules and regulations—a new list of restrictions and taboos." He said, "I am come to give you *life*." And He did not mean mere existence but life more abundant. The life He offers is not just "pie in the sky" someday. It is life here and now in this world, thirty, sixty, a hundred fold; "and in the world to come life everlasting."

Let us consider seven essentials to creative living, and then see if and how Jesus supplies these. I shall not speak of good food, minerals, vitamins, fresh air, exercise. These are obvious.

No. 1: Life must have meaning. You must have

something to live for as well as enough to live on. There is in every thinking person the need for the answer to such questions as, Where do we come from? Why are we here? Where are we going? And it is not enough just to know the meaning of life in general. Life must have meaning for you personally. You need to have the feeling that you are of value as an individual in your own right. Tragic is the life of the person who constantly says, "I'm no good. I don't count for anything. I don't see why I was ever born."

No. 2: You must believe in something. Having faith in something stable and dependent, in someone above and beyond yourself to tie to, is absolutely essential. If you cannot believe in anything, there is no security—no foundation—upon which to build.

No. 3: You must have hope for the future, with some assurance of the certainty of that future. Take out of your life all dreams of tomorrow, and what do you have left? One sure sign of old age is constantly looking back to "the good old days." To really live, you must have something to look forward to, something interesting and challenging, that has the possibility of being actually realized.

No. 4: There must be something creative to do that you enjoy doing and that you can do well. You cannot say that you are truly living, if you have nothing to do. Perhaps you have heard it said, "Oh, it is so dead around here, there is nothing to do." When you can lose yourself in some worthwhile endeavor, something that challenges the best that is in you, then you are living creatively.

No. 5: To live creatively you must act in harmony with the laws of life. To be creative in any line of work you must move and act in harmony with the laws that are involved in that area. We know this is true in electronics, physics, aviation, or any other field of science. It is just as true in other aspects of life. You cannot break these laws; you can only prove them. They break you if you violate them. And by the way, they are not superimposed upon you by a God who says, "You had better keep these laws, or I'll fix you in the judgment." No. They are great principles of life given to us in love to make life possible and meaningful.

No. 6: Satisfying, personal human relationships are necessary. When you think of the things that bring you the greatest happiness, are they not associated with persons? Are not life's greatest heartaches and deepest sorrows also involved with persons? If things are not going well at home, you cannot do your best work on the job. It is hard to study and concentrate on your assignments in school when you have been hurt by someone you love. It is only in the context of love and goodwill that one can truly get the most out of life.

No. 7: To really live, you must have within yourself power and resources adequate to meet the demands of life. You cannot live abundantly if you constantly find that you do not have within you what it takes to realize your objectives. It is terribly frustrating to have goals and never be able to reach them. To know what one ought to do, then not be able to do it, is very discouraging. Inner strength is essential to creative living. Some people are like broken cisterns—happy only when someone fills them with happiness. Their lives are full of joy for a while, but in time this leaks out, and when someone lifts the cover to look within, he finds only the spider webs and dead frogs of bitterness and self-pity inside. Others are more like bubbling fountains. They are always filling the lives of those around them with happiness. They have within them a constant supply under all circumstances. They are the people who get the most out of life. They are the ones who are truly living.

Now let us go back over these seven essentials and see if Jesus really does provide them.

First, we said that life must have meaning. You must have a sense of your own value. No teacher, no philosopher, no religious leader, gives as much meaning to life as does Jesus Christ. For Him you are of more value as an individual person than the whole world. "What shall it profit a man," said Jesus, "if he shall gain the whole world, and lose his own soul [himself]?" (Mark 8:36).

No one gives a better answer to these three questions: Where do we come from? Why are we here? Where are we going? According to Jesus, we come from the hands of a loving Creator who made us in His own image with powers akin to His own. We are here to play our part in a great drama, helping to show to the whole universe the truth about God, who has been so cruelly misrepresented by Satan. We are here to help demonstrate the contrast between the selfish way and the unselfish. And we are going to see the final triumph of God's cause in the earth. Then, being part of the Creator's family, we shall share with Him in creative activities throughout eternity. Ours is a privilege not even angels have. Surely this gives meaning and purpose to life.

Second, there must be something—someone—we can believe. There are many evidences that we can believe the Bible. In the field of archaeology we have found the Book to be a dependable authority for information on historical matters. Fulfilled prophecy gives us the assurance that God knows what He is doing. He knows what is going on and is in full control. Research in the field of science brings to light more and more evidence to support the story of Creation. And the life of Jesus has demonstrated that God is trustworthy in every area of life. We can believe in Him without wavering. These are but a few evidences that Christianity is something you can believe. To those who give Jesus a fair hearing and who are willing to follow where He leads, He validates in their own experience the truth of His words. This gives them a security that surpasses anything the world has to offer.

Third, we spoke of hope for the future. There is no hope that can compare with what Jesus offers. While the future may look dim to many people in the world, in view of the population explosion, increasing pollution, increasing crime, and the increasing danger of nuclear warfare, the Christian can recognize that his redemption is near and certain. Out of chaos, Christ will come. The world will not destroy itself in a nuclear holocaust. Jesus Himself will enter the scene and declare, "It is done." "Behold, I make all things new." Not only the world but your own personal future is in His hands, and you can trust Him. He promises to be with you always.

Fourth, Jesus' parables and Paul's writings make it very plain that you have been given gifts and talents to develop and that there is a place in God's plan in which you can use them. For you there is opportunity in fellowship with Jesus to do something creative and worthwile. Thus another essential to the abundant life is provided by Him who will help you find your place.

Fifth, we pointed out that to be creative you must carry on your activities in harmony with the laws of life. Who knows better than our Creator what these laws are? In the Ten Commandments and in the Sermon on the Mount, for example, we have them most clearly outlined. They are revealed to us in love as the great principles of life that make joy and happiness possible.

Somewhere I heard of a firm in South America that purchased a complicated piece of machinery from a company in the United States. Men from the factory installed it and gave instructions on how to make minor adjustments and repairs. After some time a breakdown occurred that the firm was unable to handle. They called the factory, and a man was dispatched immediately. When he arrived he appeared to the firm manager like a youngster just out of high school. The manager called the factory and pointed out that they had spent too much money on that equipment to let this "kid" work on it. "Please send us someone who knows his business," he insisted.

The reply was, "We sent you the best there is. We sent the inventor of the machine." Surely the One who "invented" us knows best what makes for creative living.

Sixth, since satisfying personal human relationships are so important to abundant living, surely the One who understands human hearts the best is the most appropriate counselor in this area. He alone can change the selfish heart of man, and this change is the most important factor in human relationships. The law of life is the law of love, and the principle of the Golden Rule makes possible the most satisfying life experience.

Finally, Jesus has made available to us all the power and resources of heaven. "I can do all things through Christ which strengtheneth me," said the apostle Paul. The Holy Spirit is promised to all who believe, and the love of God becomes a fountain within, overflowing in life-giving currents to others.

As the apostle Paul prays for us, he says, "I ask that your minds may be opened to see his light, so that you will know what is the hope to which he has called you, how rich are the wonderful blessings he promises his people, and how very great is his power at work in us who believe. This power working in us is the same as the mighty strength which he used when he raised Christ from death and seated him at his right side in the heavenly world" (Ephesians 1:18-20, TEV).

When Jesus said, "I am come that they might have life," He meant the abundant life available to you and to me now, as well as hereafter. Let us continue to explore how best to live that life today.

Chapter 3

Lost and Found in My Hometown

For the Son of man is come to seek and to save that which was lost (Luke 19:10).

Lost, like a gem
    That has slipped from the crown;
Lost, like a name
    Once so fair with renown;

Lost, like a sheep
    That has wandered away;
Far from the care
    Of the Shepherd, astray;

Lost, like a ship
    In the wild stormy night;
Lost without pilot,
    Or star for a light;

Lost, like a child
    From the love of the home;
Helpless, forsaken,
    In darkness to roam;

Think what it means to be lost.

Lost from the life

Only God can supply,
Lost from a place
In the palace on high,
Lost, without Christ;
Forever to die—
Think what it means to be lost.
—A. H. Ackley.*

What does it mean to be lost or saved? That is, what does it mean in terms of life where I live it here and now? To some, being lost is a matter of future destiny alone. To be on the wrong side when probation closes, to come up in the second resurrection, or to be destroyed with the wicked in the end is surely to be included with the lost. However, when Jesus said that He had come "to seek and to save that which was lost" He must have been thinking and talking about something more than future destiny, for there will be no seeking and saving after probation closes or after the final judgment. The lost condition from which Jesus would save us must include something here and now. What is it?

Let us think for a moment what it means to be lost in a sense that is not religious. I can be lost today in a number of ways:

I can be lost in the mountains or in a big city if I do not know the way home.

I can be lost in the sense of not knowing what to do next—as a student on registration day in a new school.

I can be lost if I am on the wrong road. In this instance I can be lost and not realize it.

I can be lost to a cause or an organization. One can say, "We lost a good man when Jim went to work for

---

*Copyright 1946, The Rodeheaver Co. International copyright secured. Used by permission.

our competitor."

I can be lost if I am beyond rescue, such as in a whirlpool or floating downstream too near the falls.

In the light of these different ways in which a man may be lost literally and in present tense, let us consider what it means to be lost spiritually. But first, let us define Christianity.

According to the Bible, Christianity is a fellowship—a satisfying personal love-relationship with God and our fellowmen in the great conflict between good and evil. It is therefore more a relationship with a Person than it is subscription to a creed. Creed or doctrine is important only as it affects the relationship. What you believe about a person affects your relationship with that person. What you believe about God affects your relationship with Him—whether you serve Him through fear, duty, or love, or you rebel against Him.

Notice how the apostle John puts it. He says he is writing about Jesus "so that you too may realize and enjoy fellowship as partners and partakers with us. And [this] fellowship that we have (which is a distinguishing mark of Christians) is with the Father and with His Son Jesus Christ, the Messiah" (1 John 1:3, Amplified).

According to the psalmist, life's blessings are mediated in the context of fellowship. Notice Moffatt's translation of Psalm 133: "How rare and lovely it is, this fellowship of those who meet together! . . . For in this fellowship has the Eternal fixed the blessing of an endless life."

Christianity is "the way" to this fellowship that brings true joy. As John said further: "We are now writing these things to you so that our joy [in seeing you included] may be full—and your joy may be complete" (1 John 1:4, Amplified). Christians in the days of the apostles and the early church were often referred to as those of "this way" (see Acts 9:2; 22:4).

People, then, who have not found the way to a right relationship with God or their fellowmen can in a sense be said to be lost. These are the ones Jesus came to save. To them He says, "I am the way." To those who do not know where to go or what to do, He says, "Follow me." To those on the wrong road He says, "This is the way, walk ye in it." To those who are slaves to some evil habit or caught in the grip of forces too strong for them, He says, "I will set you free." If you find that you are spending your time and talents in the cause of lesser values, Jesus says to you, " 'Go work to day in my vineyard.' I've given you talents to use for the kingdom of heaven. Go and use these to show others 'the way,' and I will be with you forever."

Notice that Jesus said, "I *am* the way, the truth, and the life" (John 14:6). He didn't just say, "I am *telling* you the way." He *is* the way. He wants us to know that in fellowship with Him we can not only find the right way but also find the courage and strength to walk in it. Thus Jesus is not up there on top of the stairs saying to me, "Come on up, Paul. If you can make it, we will have a good time." He is saying instead, "Paul, I'm coming down to where you are, and we will climb the steps together." That makes a world of difference, doesn't it?

Suppose I am lost in the woods. Finally I come across an old mountaineer. When I tell him about my predicament, he assures me that he knows every canyon and trail in the area and that he will guide me home. Am I lost any longer? No. Am I home? Of course not. I may have a long way to go, but I am not lost as long as I stay close to the old mountaineer and follow where he leads. So it is if we keep close to Jesus Christ and follow where He leads. In fellowship with Him all our needs will be supplied, and He will see that we get home. He will never leave us or forsake us. It is only when we leave Him and go our own way that we get lost again. If the old mountaineer leads down a particular trail, and we don't want to follow him in that direction, obviously we can't expect him to take us home.

You may say, "That sounds simple enough, but Jesus is not as real to me as an old mountaineer." This is true for most of us. Comprehending the reality of Jesus seems to be easier for children because of their vivid imaginations. As we grow older, we seem to become more skeptical, and at times the reality of the spiritual world is eclipsed. However, the more you read and think about Him and the more you pray about it, the more real He will become to you. By His Holy Spirit He will speak to you personally. Of this we shall say more later—particularly in the two chapters on prayer.

Talking about being lost and found in the way mentioned above is just another way of talking about sin and salvation. When you think of Christianity as a love-relationship with God and your fellowmen, sin has to do with broken relations and all the tragic results that follow. Salvation comes through the restoration of those relationships. This is the atonement—the at-one-ment—about which the Bible speaks. Let us look at it from this point of view.

We are told, " 'None of us liveth to himself.' Romans 14:7. This is a law of God in heaven and on earth. God is the great center. From Him all life proceeds. To Him all service, homage, and allegiance belong. For all created beings there is the one great principle of life—dependence upon and co-operation with God" (*Testimonies for the Church*, Vol. 6, p. 236). Let us draw a picture of this. Print the word *GOD* in capital letters, and surround it with a circle of capital *I*'s, like this:

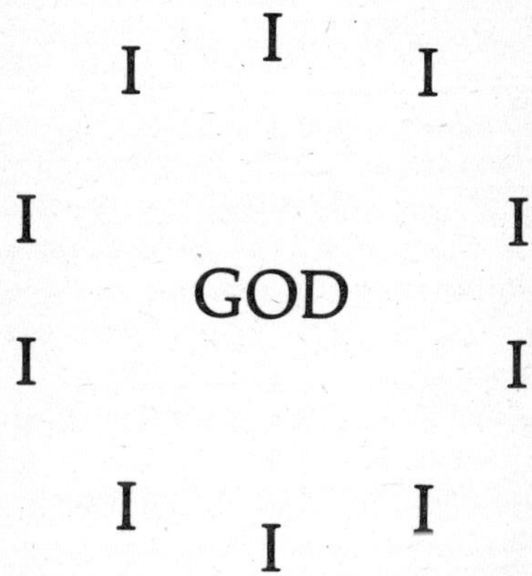

God is the only one who has life in Himself. He is the Source of life, and He alone can say, "I am." Because He is a God of love, He wants beings to love and to be loved. He therefore created them with powers akin to His own so that they could respond to His love. The *I*'s in the circle represent the individuals in God's family who are dependent upon Him for life. In the context of love for their Creator and for each other, there is joy and gladness, creativity and fulfillment, and all that bring happiness and satisfaction to the persons involved. God gets His pleasure from the happiness of His creatures, and the law of life for earth and heaven, which makes happiness possible, is the law of unselfish love. No one lives to himself.

This is true of God's family on earth. "Under God, Adam was to stand at the head of the earthly family to maintain the principles of the heavenly family. This would have brought peace and happiness. But the law that none 'liveth to himself' Satan was determined to oppose. He desired to live for self. He sought to make himself a center of influence. It was this that incited rebellion in heaven" (*ibid.*).

In the beginning, "God saw every thing that he had made, and, behold, it was very good" (Genesis 1:31). And so it was, until one of His created beings, Lucifer, decided to rebel against the God-centered way of living and to make himself a center. This is how he became Satan. He declared that God was selfish, demanding, and unjust in requiring obedience to His laws. He persuaded one third of those in his immediate locale—the angels—to follow him. Picture him to one side with his followers around him:

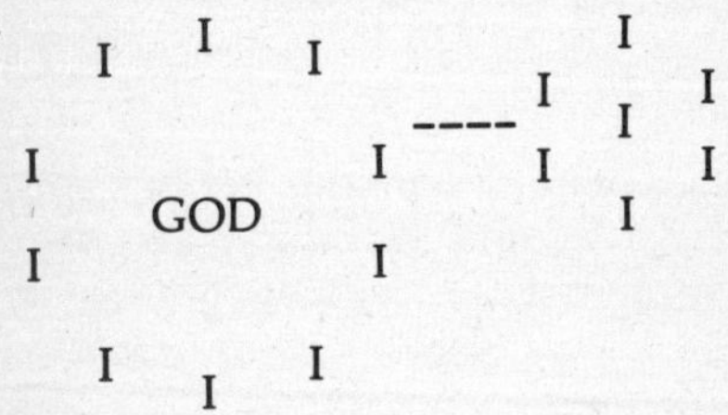

Soon Satan persuaded Adam—the newly created member of God's family on earth—to believe him rather than his Creator. Thus man's loving, trusting relationship with God was broken. He separated himself from God's family circle, and tragic results followed.

Notice the steps in this separation. First there was

distrust of God. This led to disobedience, and broken relationships followed. Not only was man afraid of God, but soon it became apparent that this affected his relations with his fellowmen as well. In the very first family one brother hated and killed another. You see, there can be no true brotherhood of man without the Fatherhood of God. You can have no brothers without a father.

Because of the separation from God through distrust and disobedience—this is what the Bible calls sin—man becomes self-centered and experiences loneliness, fear and anxiety, guilt, hatred and hostility, envy and strife, pride, frustration, disease and death, with all the heartache and suffering that accompany these. This is a picture of the lost condition of man. Let us add these facts to our diagram:

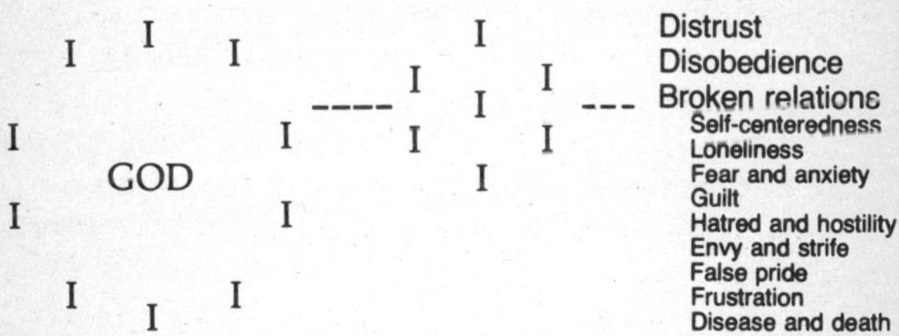

What is now the remedy? "Who could . . . counterwork the plans of Satan and bring the world back to its loyalty? God said: 'I will send My Son.' . . . [Quotes John 3:16.] This is the remedy for sin. Christ says: 'Where Satan has set his throne, there shall stand My cross. Satan shall be cast out, and I will be lifted up to draw all men unto Me. I will become the center of the redeemed world' " (*ibid.*, pp. 236, 237). To self-centered man in his loneliness and lost condition, Jesus says, "Return to your center—God" (*ibid.*, p. 237).

The remedy, then, is to get back to a right relationship with God first of all. A God-centered love relationship is man's only hope. How is this to be brought about? We looked at the steps away from that relationship. Let us now look at the steps back.

Since distrust was the first step away, the restoration of trust must be the first step back. With trust and faith reestablished, obedience will follow in the place of disobedience, and restored relations will result. Then instead of being self-centered, man will become God-centered. Fellowship will take the place of loneliness, peace and security will replace fear and anxiety, the guilty will experience forgiveness, love and goodwill will cancel hatred and hostility, and envy and strife will give way to concern for others. In place of pride, man will have true self-respect, fulfillment will be known instead of frustration, and disease and death will give way to healing and eternal life.

What makes all this possible? The life and death of Jesus Christ. In Jesus' life on earth, His death on the cross, and His resurrection, we see demonstrated the contrast between Satan's way and God's way. There, Satan's accusations against God were proved false, and God is seen to be the trustworthy, loving heavenly Father that He really is. He is not a selfish God. He is Himself the personification of the law of self-sacrificing love. He is not a bloodthirsty God demanding a sacrifice; He is Himself the sacrifice. The cross demonstrated this.

Let us now complete our diagram. To the right of the word *distrust* put a capital *I* to represent lost man. Above this *I* put a cross. Then, because of the cross and all that it symbolizes, we can put opposite distrust, trust and faith; opposite disobedience, obedience; and so on. Now look at the diagram as a whole.

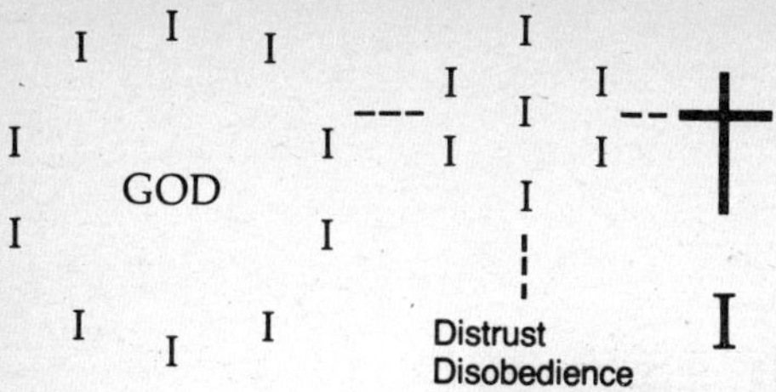

Distrust
Disobedience
Broken relations
- Self-centeredness
- Loneliness
- Fear and anxiety
- Guilt
- Hatred and hostility
- Envy and strife
- False pride
- Frustration
- Disease and death

Trust and faith
Obedience
Restored relations
- God-centeredness
- Fellowship
- Peace and security
- Forgiveness
- Love and goodwill
- Concern for others
- True self-respect
- Fulfillment
- Healing and eternal life

All the evidence of God's trustworthiness is now available to everyone. All God asks is that we trust Him enough to follow where He leads, and He will restore all that is lost. In fellowship with Him and willingness to do what He says, we are no longer lost. In this restored relationship we are saved.

Chapter 4

"Mamma, Where Is God?"

O God, thou art my God; early will I seek thee: my soul thirsteth for thee, my flesh longeth for thee in a dry and thirsty land, where no water is (Psalm 63:1).

And ye shall seek me, and find me, when ye shall search for me with all your heart (Jeremiah 29:13).

And Enoch walked with God (Genesis 5:24).

Sunlight, mountain peaks etched against the sky,
Cool breeze, snowy clouds floating lazily by;
Green vale, cottage white; rippling, singing brook,
Tall trees, weeping boughs, cool and shady nook.
Blue lake, bluer sky, birds swift on the wing,
White sail, beach of sand, a playground for a king.
Twilight, shadows fall; workers homeward plod;
Contentment, beauty; I've spent the day with God!
—Madoline E. Sterling.

A beautiful thought—these words of the poet. So often we enjoy the beautiful, taking it all for granted, and forget God, the Creator of the beautiful. "I've spent the day with God," she said. What if that day had been filled with tragedy? Could she still say it? Here is another poem:

We were resting awhile in a valley
With flowers everywhere,
Bluebirds singing in the trees

Amid a perfume rare.

A great range of mountains
Hemmed the valley in,
Shutting out the rest of the world
With all its strife and din.

And all day long on the mountain
A storm raged at the peak.
Lightning and thunder flashed and rolled
As if playing hide and seek.

My imagination pictured God
Walking in the cloud
To the roll of a mighty organ
As the thunder crashed so loud.

And just as the sun was setting,
The great clouds sailed away.
The mountain peak was clothed in snow
Where the storm had raged all day.

And I love to think God was there,
Walking in the storm,
And the snow that on the mountain lay
Was the cloak He dropped from His arm.
—Verna Kindig.

Shutting out the rest of the world with all its strife and din, resting in the quiet valley with its flowers and singing birds, we watch a storm on the the mountaintop and think God is walking in the storm. I imagine David had the same feeling when he wrote Psalm 29. Read it sometime—his description of God in a storm. But there are three questions to think about while we consider fellowship with God as necessary to salvation. In the last chapter we spoke of this in terms of staying by the old mountaineer.

Question No. 1: Where is God? Is He with the poet in the beautiful valley, or is He in the storm on the mountaintop? What if the storm should move down into the valley in the form of a hurricane or tornado, then where is God?

Question No. 2: Are all storms "acts of God"?

Question No. 3: What does it mean to walk with God? How can it be said of us in this generation, as it was said of Enoch and Noah and others, "They walked with God"?

Some time ago I heard of the following experience of a mother and her little daughter:

"Mamma, where is God?"

"God is up in heaven, dear."

"Then He can't see me, can He?"

"Oh, yes, He can, honey; God is everywhere."

Some time later: "Mamma, I've looked everywhere, and I can't find God anywhere." After some hesitation, Mother replied, "Well, dear, He is inside of you."

A few days later the mother was expecting guests for dinner in the evening, and early in the day she placed on the dining room table a bowl of fruit, beautifully arranged and decorated with greenery. Jane was told not to touch it because it was "for company," and Mother wanted it to look nice until the close of the meal. While the mother was in town that afternoon, Jane came in from play, and there in front of her set the tempting bowl of fruit. She was hungry. Deciding that she could take the little red apple on one side and rearrange the greenery a bit without her mother noticing it, she took and ate it. When her mother discovered that the apple was missing, Jane was duly reprimanded.

"But how do you know I took it, Mother? You

didn't see me, did you?"

"No I didn't, but God saw you, Jane."

"No He didn't. I closed my eyes, and He couldn't see out. You said He was inside of me."

We smile, but even children want to know about God. A little boy was peeking through the opening in a great cathedral door, which stood just a little ajar. When the caretaker approached, the little fellow said, "Say, mister, is God in there?"

Where is God? Actually God is everywhere. In Psalm 139 David describes this so beautifully: "Whither shall I go from thy spirit? or whither shall I flee from thy presence? If I ascend up into heaven, thou art there: if I make my bed in hell, behold, thou art there. If I take the wings of the morning, and dwell in the uttermost parts of the sea; even there shall thy hand lead me, and thy right hand shall hold me" (verses 7-10).

The apostle Paul tells us that "in him we live, and move, and have our being" (Acts 17:28). God is therefore not only within us, but He is both in the quiet valley and in the storm on the mountaintop.

By the way, the storm on the mountaintop makes possible the watering of the flowers in the valley. Often life is like that too. There are times when God seems lionlike and cruel—walking in the storm. Note a picture of God in Isaiah: "For thus hath the Lord spoken unto me, Like as the lion and the young lion roaring on his prey, when a multitude of shepherds is called forth against him, he will not be afraid of their voice, nor abase himself for the noise of them: so shall the Lord of hosts come down to fight for mount Zion, and for the hill thereof" (Isaiah 31:4).

God is here pictured as a lion roaring on his prey. I would have written it differently. I would have God as a shepherd with a lamb in His arms and the lions roaring around Him. But no, the prophet pictures it the other way. And that is the way it seems at times. However, the more you think about it, the more you realize that there are times when we need a God like that—lionlike and strong.

But note the beautifully contrasting picture of God in the next verse: "As birds flying, so will the Lord of hosts defend Jerusalem." In the Hebrew, the word *birds* is diminutive and feminine. "As birds flying" could be translated: "As little mother birds hovering." During those times when God seems like a lion roaring over his prey, if you could catch a glimpse of His heart, you would discover that He is as tender and loving as a little mother bird. That is the kind of God He is.

To the question, "Are *all* storms acts of God?" the answer is, No. The prince of the power of the air, to whom Adam sold his dominion, is responsible for destructive storms in spite of the fact that insurance companies call them acts of God. "Satan works through the elements. . . . Even now he is at work. In accidents and calamities by sea and by land, in great conflagrations, in fierce tornadoes and terrific hailstorms, in tempests, floods, cyclones, tidal waves, and earthquakes, in every place and in a thousand forms" (*The Great Controversy*, pp. 589, 590). Who is at work? Satan is at work. "Satan is the destroyer; God is the restorer" (*The Ministry of Healing*, p. 113).

Death and destruction are the result of sin. But even there, God is in control. He says, "Thus far and no farther." Not everything that happens is God's will, but nothing can happen to defeat His will.

Whether in the valley or on the mountaintop, God is with us. Take note of the following promises:

"The Lord is nigh unto them that are of a broken heart; and saveth such as be of a contrite spirit" (Psalm 34:18).

"The Lord is nigh unto all them that call upon him, to all that call upon him in truth" (Psalm 145:18).

"When thou passet through the waters, I will be with thee" (Isaiah 43:2).

"Lo, I am with you alway, even unto the end of the world" (Matthew 28:20).

"I will never leave thee, nor forsake thee. So that we may boldly say, The Lord is my helper, and I will not fear" (Hebrews 13:5, 6).

The secret of living a Christian life is nicely stated in Micah 6:8: "He has showed you, O man, what is good. And what does the Lord require of you? To act justly and to love mercy and to walk humbly with your God" (NIV).

What does it mean to walk with God? How is it done? Those who cultivate the consciousness of His presence walk with Him. Those who agree with God walk with Him. "Can two walk together, except they be agreed?" (Amos 3:3). The ones who seek to please God walk with Him. "By faith Enoch was translated; . . . he had this testimony, that he pleased God" (Hebrews 11:5). It was by faith that Enoch walked with God. Those who love God, who trust Him completely, who have confidence enough to follow where He leads, and who recognize that they are partners with God in every worthwhile endeavor—these are the ones who walk with God.

You see, God wants the fellowship of free man, not puppets. While it is true that in Him we live and move and have our being, yet He made us free moral persons and He wants us to walk with Him by choice. He therefore does all He can to persuade us to seek Him and to learn more about Him so that we can prepare for eternal fellowship with Him.

Who then walks with God?

The farmer who sows, cultivates, and waters, watching God give the increase.

The biologist who sees God's handiwork in all the living things in the field.

The research scientist who recognizes God's doings in the laboratory.

The astronomer who measures the movements of heavenly bodies and notes the wisdom and power of God.

The businessman who remembers God's ownership of all things and that he is but a steward.

The historian who traces the hand of God in history.

The political scientist who knows that righteousness exalts a nation.

The college teacher or student who recognizes that the fear of the Lord is the beginning of wisdom.

The lawyer who believes that on the two commandments of love to God and man hang all law and order.

The common laborer who does his job as unto the Lord.

The builder who realizes that "except the Lord build the house, they labour in vain that build it."

The housewife and mother whose highest aim is to create in her home an atmosphere of love and good cheer and to make of it a little sanctuary, hallowed by the presence of the Divine One.

The musician whose talent is used to lift men into the atmosphere of heaven.

The artist who captures a new glimpse of the glory of God and with a brush spreads it across the canvas for all to see.

All of these walk with God. But most of all, regardless of his vocation, he walks with God who stoops to ease a neighbor's burden or to meet some fellow traveler's need.

If you would find the Master in order to walk with Him, you must search for Him where He is.

I sought the Pearl of greatest price,
Midst costly jewels shining
With ruby, sapphire, amethyst,
Enhanced by silken lining.
By works of art, and treasures rare
I searched, but never found it there.

I sought it long by land and sea,
In many a town and city,
Within the haunts of wealthy men,
Or dancers, gay and pretty.
Nor student versed in letters Greek,
Who yet directed where to seek.

I turned at length to home again,
To serve with humble people,
To learn that God was not confined
In church or tower or steeple.
I stooped to ease a neighbor's care,
And lo, the Pearl of Price was there.

—Brenda Heaton.

Those who walk with God will be taken "home" in the end, just as were Enoch, Elijah, and Moses. If alive when Jesus comes, they will be translated. If asleep in death, they will be resurrected. This is what Christianity is all about.

Chapter 5

Good News

Be not afraid; for behold, I bring you good news of a great joy which will come to all the people (Luke 2:10, RSV).

Then I saw another angel flying high in the air, with an eternal message of Good News to announce to the peoples of the earth, to every race, tribe, language, and nation (Revelation 14:6, TEV).

"If only I hadn't heard about Seventh-day Adventists, I wouldn't have to live their teachings; but now that I am convinced they are right, I am obligated to do so. I don't want to burn, so here goes." What a motive for Christian living! Have you ever felt that way? Is the Christian message as taught by Seventh-day Adventists good news to you?

Good news for most of us is something to be excited about. You feel like shouting it for all to hear. "Our new car will be ready tomorrow!" "I received my acceptance to medical school!" "The war is over!" "George is coming home tomorrow!" "She said yes!" "It's a boy!" The word *gospel* means "good news." Is it that to you?

How about the three angels' messages of Revelation 14? The first angel is said to have everlasting good news to announce to all the world. He then proclaims: "Fear God, and give glory to him; for the hour of his judgment is come: and worship him that made heaven, and earth, and the sea, and the fountains of waters" (verse 7). Is this good news to you? Or do you see only a diagram of the 2300 days and a fearful looking forward to the judgment, with the anxious thought: "What if my name should come up today?"

The second angel announces the fall of Babylon, and the third warns against the worship of the beast and his image under pain of the "wrath of God" and eternal fire. What kind of good news is this to you?

According to John, these three angels' messages are the last to be given to the world. Following their proclamation, Jesus comes in the clouds of heaven. Obviously they are important. What do they mean? In what way are they good news?

Let us take another look at the first angel's declaration. He admonishes us to "fear God, and give glory to him; for the hour of his judgment is come." We understand that the hour of His judgment began in 1844. This is based on the prophecy of Daniel in chapters 8 and 9. The verse that establishes the date is Daniel 8:14: "Unto two thousand and three hundred days; then shall the sanctuary be cleansed." Do you remember that this statement is given in answer to a question? Go back and read the chapter again with this thought in mind. What question does it answer?

Daniel had seen for the third time a panorama of history, with the rise and fall of nations and all the heartache and suffering associated with war. He saw Error sit enthroned and Truth trampled underfoot. He saw a power magnify itself above Christ. He saw many good people destroyed. He saw deception and arrogance prosper. Then he heard one saint speaking to another, echoing the outcry of every thoughtful person through the ages, "How long is this going to continue?" And I am sure in their minds was the question, "How can God be a God of love and allow this to go on so long? If He is all-wise and all-powerful, and if He really loves people, why doesn't He do something about it?" The answer was: "Unto two thousand and three hundred days; then shall the sanctuary be cleansed."

To us at first that seems to be a strange answer. What has the cleansing of the sanctuary to do with it? The sanctuary, of course, is in heaven, God's dwelling place, the headquarters of His government. What needs cleansing there? The word *cleansed* used in this passage comes from the Hebrew word *ṣadaq*, which means "vindicated" or "justified." The same word is used in Genesis 44:16, where Judah makes his speech before Joseph when the silver cup was found in Benjamin's possession. Judah says, "What shall we say? . . . how shall we clear ourselves?" The expression "clear ourselves" is the Hebrew word *ṣadaq*. It has also been translated "restored to its rightful state." With this in mind, the answer to the question asked then is, "Unto 2300 days (years), then shall Heaven be vindicated." Since a day stands for a year in this Bible prophecy, the time period here reaches from the command to restore and rebuild Jerusalem in 457 BC to the year AD 1844. In other words, in 1844 a movement began, both in heaven and on earth, that would justify God and vindicate His character. Then it would be seen how God could be a God of love and put up with all the tragedy involved and also that He would do something about it. In heaven the great investigative judgment would begin. On earth a people would arise who would proclaim to all the world the truth about God.

In the beginning of the great controversy between

good and evil, Satan brought "lying charges against the divine character and government. . . . He . . . accused God of seeking merely the exaltation of Himself in requiring submission and obedience from His creatures" (*The Great Controversy*, p. 502). And ever since, He has sought to give men a false concept of God. He led "men to look upon God as the author of sin, and suffering, and death" (*The Desire of Ages*, p. 24). His own acts of cruelty in nature he would lead men to believe were God's doing. He took the truth that "the wages of sin is death" and twisted it to read in men's minds that "the wages of God is death." "Satan works through the elements. . . . Even now he is at work. In accidents and calamities by sea and by land, in great conflagrations, in fierce tornadoes and terrific hailstorms, in tempests, floods, cyclones, tidal waves, and earthquakes, in every place" (*The Great Controversy*, pp. 589, 590). Insurance companies call these "acts of God."

"With his own evil characteristics he [Satan] sought to invest the loving Creator. Thus he deceived angels. Thus he deceived men. He led them to doubt the word of God, and to distrust His goodness. Because God is a God of justice and terrible majesty, Satan caused them to look upon Him as severe and unforgiving. Thus he drew men to join him in rebellion against God, and the night of woe settled down upon the world" (*The Desire of Ages*, p. 22).

The Good News is that God is not like that. God could afford to be misunderstood through the years in order to let Satan's character and way be fully demonstrated. But now the time has come to get the truth before the world that God is not the kind of person Satan has made Him out to be. God is like Jesus. He is loving and kind and forgiving. He is also just. He will bring justice to earth. Enthroned Error will fall. Evil will be punished in the end. But best of all, those who believe in Him will have everlasting life in a world—this world made new—in which there will be no more suffering.

This is what the first angel means when he says, "Give glory to . . . [God]." His glory is His character. The truth to be given to the world is the truth of His righteousness. Paul says concerning the gospel, "Therein is the righteousness of God revealed" (Romans 1:17). The "glory of God" is revealed "in the face of Jesus Christ" (2 Corinthians 4:6). God's righteousness is there revealed.

But perhaps you are thinking of the word *judgment* and the statements of the second and third angels. God is a God of judgment because He uses good judgment in all that He does. Isn't that good news? When you think of Babylon as a symbol of all the powers of evil that seek to destroy God's people and that seem to prosper in the world, isn't it good news to hear that they will fall someday? God is a loving God who is also just and righteous.

Do you begin to see why the three angels' messages are good news to get excited about? Note the following statement by Ellen G. White:

"The message of Christ's righteousness is to sound from one end of the earth to the other to prepare the way of the Lord. This is the glory of God, which closes the work of the third angel. . . .

"The truths of the third angel's message [which includes all three] have been presented by some as a dry theory, but in this message is to be presented Christ the Living One. . . . Through this message the character of God in Christ is to be manifested to the world" (*Testimonies for the Church*, Vol. 6, pp. 19, 20).

When we see Wrong enthroned and Evil prosper while Truth is trampled underfoot, the good news is that in the end justice will triumph.

Facing the judgment is good news only when you know the Judge, who loves you very much, and when you know that He always uses good judgment in all His decisions.

To understand even better the Good News, let us next take a look at the cross.

Chapter 6

The Scandal and Glory of the Cross

God forbid that I should glory, save in the cross of our Lord Jesus Christ (Galatians 6:14).

I determined not to know any thing among you, save Jesus Christ, and him crucified (1 Corinthians 2:2).

We preach Christ, the Messiah, crucified, which to the Jews is a scandal and an offensive stumbling block, . . . and to the Gentiles it is absurd and utterly unphilosophical nonsense (1 Corinthians 1:23, Amplified).

And I, if I be lifted up from the earth, will draw all men unto me (John 12:32).

What is the drawing power of the cross? How could anyone ever be attracted to such an instrument of torture? Was it necessary for Jesus to die? Why? Who, or what, demanded it?

The Bible says, "Without the shedding of blood there is no forgiveness of sins" (Hebrews 9:22, RSV). Why is this true? Is God a "bloodthirsty" deity demanding the blood of the sinner? If it were not for Jesus, who shed *His* blood for our sins, would it just be too bad for us?

On one occasion a woman brought her husband into my office and said, "My husband wants Bible studies." There was something about the way she said it and what seemed to be his reaction that caused me to think she wanted him to have the studies. Anyway, we made an appointment.

On the day he was to come to my office after his work, I called his wife and asked her to let him come alone so that we could talk man to man. When the time came he arrived, and after a few minutes of conversation getting acquainted, I said to him, "I have a sneaking suspicion that your wife wants you to have these Bible studies."

He smiled a bit and then sobered as he said, "To tell you the truth, Yes. It is my last attempt to save our marriage." But then he hastened to add, "Now don't get me wrong. I think the Bible is a wonderful book, and I like the Sermon on the Mount and the parables of Jesus, but I never could be a Christian."

"What makes you say that?" I asked.

"Well, for one thing, there is too much blood in your Christianity."

This was near the Easter weekend, and he referred to the many pictures around of Christ on the cross and the shedding of His blood. Then he continued, "I attended your Sunday School—oh, I beg your pardon, I mean your Saturday School—the other day, and just like all the others I have attended, even your songs are dripping with blood."

Stop and think a moment. What about some of the songs we sing? "There Is Power in the Blood," "Redeemed by the Blood of the Lamb," "There Is a Fountain Filled With Blood." What do these songs mean to you? Why all this blood?

Another man said to me one day when I invited him to attend our church, "I never could be an Adventist."

"Why not?" I asked.

"Well, for one thing," he said, "you believe the

Old Testament as well as the New, don't you?"

"Yes," I said, "we believe that God has spoken to us all through the Bible."

"That is the trouble," he replied. "To me, the God of the Old Testament is not the same God Jesus talked about as our heavenly Father. I happened to be reading about the dedication of Solomon's temple the other day, and it mentioned the fact that some 120,000 sheep and 22,000 oxen were slaughtered as a sacrifice to God, and the offerings were said to be 'a sweet-smelling savour' unto the Lord. Jesus spoke of a God who is concerned about even a sparrow."

What would you say to him? What would you say to the man whose wife wanted him to have the Bible studies?

How can the story of the cross be Good News? The apostle Paul speaks of *glorying* in the cross. To glory in something is to boast about it, to exult with joy or triumph. Words like *praise, honor, distinction, renown,* and *splendor* are associated with the word *glory*. Something is glorious when it exhibits attitudes, qualities, or acts that are praiseworthy—something resplendent, magnificent, brilliant, and outstanding. How in the world can a cross be such?

Even Paul admitted that it was a scandal to the Jews and nonsense to the Greeks.

For the Jew, how could a crucified man be the Messiah? Moses said, "Cursed is every one that hangeth on a tree" (Galatians 3:13; cf. Deuteronomy 21:22, 23). How could a man, cursed of God, be the world's Redeemer? The cross was a symbol of weakness and defeat. If they tried to crucify the true Messiah, God would surely take the situation in hand. Even a child would think so. A little boy for the first time saw a picture of Christ crucified. When his parents explained to him what it was all about, he said, "Well, if God had been there, He wouldn't have let them do it, would he, Dad?"

To the Greek the cross was altogether foolishness. It would be sheer absurdity to think that the Saviour of the world would be a crucified criminal. A super Aristotle, a resurrected Mystery Divinity of some kind, or a secret astrological gnosis might be, yes. But this crucified man? No! Don't insult my intelligence.

In Paul's day the Jews believed that God was sovereign. He could bring order out of chaos. If this was true of God, He would do something about our situation. They did recognize the power of the demoniac, but God was still supreme. They demanded action. "Give us a sign," they said, "not just a proposition to argue about."

The Greeks, on the other hand, sought wisdom. A rational explanation was needed, a new philosophy. Correct intellectual formulas—logical positivism were demanded. Logical and psychological analysis was necessary to their minds.

In our time the Hebrew and Greek minds converge. Modern Western civilization especially is characterized by both. And so two demands—action and explanation—are made upon God today. "If God is sovereign, let Him do something"; and, "If only there were sense to it, or meaning to life."

Now according to Paul, God has on the cross met both demands. Both God's power and His wisdom are revealed there, "both [for] Jews and Greeks, Christ the power of God, and the wisdom of God" (1 Corinthians 1:24).

We have noted briefly the scandal of the cross from both the Jewish and Greek points of view. There is even a so-called Christian point of view that truly scandalizes the name of God and is just as unreasonable as either of the first two. It is absolutely pagan in nature and causes intelligent people to reject the gospel completely. The question is: "How can a God of love demand the death of Christ in order to forgive men their sins on the one hand and then condemn a whole race—the Jewish race—for killing Him on the other? If the death of Christ was necessary to reconcile man to God and God to man, and therefore necessary for this reason for man's salvation, did not Satan do us a favor by bringing about the Crucifixion? " One can see in the cross a picture of a tyrannical God demanding the blood of the sinner and a loving Saviour who offers to shed His blood instead. This is a tragedy.

What, now, is the answer? What is the glory of the cross?

Obviously it is not the cross but the glorious character of the Christ of the cross that makes this symbol so meaningful. The event becomes a high moment in history because of the greatness of the Man involved and what He accomplished there. We can properly assess it only when we understand what needs were met. Only as we see how immensely exacting and how many sided His work has been can we be truly impressed.

Let us look at the cross then, in the light of the greatness of the Man upon it. His greatness becomes manifest in the light of the great controversy between good and evil and the issues at stake—why He is there and what the results will be to God and man.

In the beginning God created a perfect universe. All things animate and inanimate were in perfect harmony with His will. And His will was the happiness of His creatures, which brought Him happiness and joy in return. There were perfect confidence and trust, with loyalty and love, among the creatures and between them and their Creator. All creation sang for joy.

But when sin entered, all this changed. No longer were all His creatures in perfect harmony with His will. God had a rebellion on His hands. Man lost confidence in God. He believed God's enemy instead. God no longer could trust man. God had to keep him from the tree of life. Choosing to separate himself from God, man broke communication with his Creator, and the human race became more and more ignorant of God. Man's broken relationship with God resulted in broken relations with his fellowmen, bringing suspicion and hatred. Cain murdered Abel, and in due time there was complete confusion at Babel.

When man was cut off from the Source of life, sorrow, suffering, disease, and death followed. These are the results of sin to man. And the result to God? He is misrepresented and misunderstood. Disharmony exists in His world, and the loss of fellowship with His created loved ones brings sorrow to His great heart of love.

What now needs to be done?

The truth about God needs to be revealed.

Satan's deceptions need to be unmasked.

Forgiveness and new birth need to be provided for man.

It needs to be demonstrated that God is still sovereign, that God is love, that man can please God and conform perfectly to His will, and that this is the way to true freedom and peace.

It must also be shown that Satan's way is the way of suffering and death. The contrast needs to be seen. Note the following statement:

"The earth was dark through misapprehension of God. That the gloomy shadows might be lightened, that the world might be brought back to God, Satan's deceptive power was to be broken. This could not be done by force. The exercise of force is contrary to the principles of God's government; He desires only the service of love; and love cannot be commanded; it cannot be won by force or authority. Only by love is love awakened. To know God is to love Him; His character must be manifested in contrast to the character of Satan. This work only one Being in all the universe could do. Only He who knew the height and depth of the love of God could make it known. Upon the world's dark night the Sun of Righteousness must rise, 'with healing in His wings.' Mal. 4:2" (*The Desire of Ages,* p. 22).

There needs to be the restoration of communication and confidence. Some questions need to be answered. Barriers need to be broken down. Atonement is needed that all my be one again.

The greatness of Christ is revealed in how completely and beautifully He, the Man of the cross, meets these needs and successfully accomplishes His work. Just before He was crucified, He said, "I have finished the work which thou gavest me to do," and on the cross He cried out, "It is finished"!

In this God-man, Jesus Christ, heaven and earth are reunited, and in Him men are reunited. In Him the truth about God is revealed, for He was "God . . . manifest in the flesh." He was "the express image of his [Father's] person." Here is what God is really like.

Christ also revealed in His life and work that God is still sovereign. The miracles He performed demonstrated this. Men could see His power over the forces of nature and over the forces of evil and death.

On the cross you see, not a bloodthirsty God demanding the blood of the sinner—demanding a sacrifice—but a God who is Himself the sacrifice, Himself the personification of the law of self-sacrificing love. God does not love us because Jesus gave His life for us. He gave His Son, Jesus, because He loves us. What a difference! When John the Baptist introduced Jesus to the people he said, "Behold the Lamb of God, which taketh away the sin of the world" (John 1:29).

But what about the blood? What could I say to the men who spoke of so much blood in Christianity? Satan would like for us to see only *death* in that symbol. May I suggest that the blood is more a symbol of *life*. "The life of every living thing is in the blood" (Leviticus 17:11, TEV). "As for the life of all flesh, the blood of it represents the life of it" (Leviticus 17:14, Amplified).

Actually the *life* of Christ is far more important than His death for our salvation. I am not saying His death was unimportant. He died for a number of reasons that I will mention later, but were it not for His sinless life before He died, His death would have been the result only of His own sin and would not have helped us at all. And were it not for His resurrection—His life after His death—our faith would be in vain as well. The apostle Paul tells us, "If Christ has not been raised, then your faith is a delusion and you are still lost in your sins. It would also mean that the believers in Christ who have died are lost. . . . But the truth is that Christ has been raised from death, as the guarantee that those who sleep in death will also be raised" (1 Corinthians 15:17-20, TEV).

The blood best symbolizes His life, which He lived for us, which He gave for us, and which He lives for us and in us now. Thus when I sing "Redeemed by the blood" and "There is power in the blood" I see the redemption and the power in the *life* of Christ.

Why then was His death necessary? Why is it that "without the shedding of blood there is no forgiveness of sins" (Hebrews 9:22, RSV)? It means "without the sharing of a life, there is no forgiveness." And it means more. The nature of the great controversy and the stability of the universe made this death necessary. The security of the universe was at stake. It is not enough only to know that God is love. For security there must be orderliness. Causes and effects must be dependable. If the wages of sin is death in its very nature, God could not be just and excuse it. If He could forgive sin simply by canceling it, one could conclude that it was not very important. The only way forgiveness is possible is for God Himself to take on the results to show that the effect of sin really is death. Then the seriousness of sin would be revealed, and forgiveness would show both His justice and His love, both of which were challenged by Satan. This is why God gave His Son to die: "to declare . . . his righteousness: that he might be just, and the justifier of him which believeth in Jesus" (Romans 3:26).

On the cross you also see the character of Satan unmasked. Intelligent beings see what selfishness and sin do to a being as brilliant as Lucifer. It blinds him to his own limitations. He thinks he is better than his Creator. In fact, it even leads him to seek to destroy his Creator. The universe watches as he takes the hands of Jesus that have been outstretched in blessings only and nails them to the cross. That is what sin does. The contrast between Satan's way and God's becomes clear.

Everything that needed to be done to restore the confidence of heavenly beings was completed at the cross, and men can be forgiven. In fellowship with Christ men can be transformed and united. Joined with Christ, men can live in conformity to God's will, and they are set free. Christ's defeat of Satan was comprehensive and complete. Paul describes this victory thus: "On that cross he discarded the cosmic powers and authorities like a garment; he made a public spectacle of them and led them as captives in his triumphal procession" (Colossians 2:15, NEB).

How did He do this? You see, evil is self-propelling and leads to greater evils. This is the devil's strategy. God outmaneuvered evil by meeting it, not with force or violence, but with love, and thus He broke the vicious cycle, offering forgiveness rather than revenge. "Instead of destroying the world, God sent His Son to save it" (*The Desire of Ages*, p. 37).

Here was action and power on the one hand, and superior wisdom on the other—the action and power and wisdom of true love. God is transcendent after all. He does not stoop to follow Satan's strategy. No wonder, on seeing in vision the marks of the Crucifixion at the second coming of Christ, Habakkuk said, "There was the hiding of his power" (Habakkuk 3:4).

Wherein, then, is the power and glory of the cross? It is in the power and glory of the Man on the cross. Seen in its true perspective, it is at least sevenfold:

1. the compelling power of love;
2. the kingly power of reason;
3. the stabilizing power of justice;
4. the releasing power of true freedom;
5. the transforming power of fellowship with Christ;

6. the healing power of redemption, of forgiveness, of sanctification;
7. the creative power of the dedicated life—a noble purpose—a magnificent obsession.

When I survey the wondrous cross
    On which the Prince of glory died,
My richest gain I count but loss,
    And pour contempt on all my pride.

Were the whole realm of nature mine,
    That were a tribute far too small;
Love so amazing, so divine,
    Demands my life, my soul, my all.

—Isaac Watts.

Chapter 7

Three Men Meet Jesus

Sir, we would see Jesus (John 12:21).

And when they saw him, they worshipped him (Matthew 28:17).

Show me Thy face.
One transit gleam of loveliness divine,
And I shall never think or dream
Of other love than Thine.

—Selected.

Valentine Burke was his name. Lucas A. Reed in his book, *Buried Treasure,* tells his story something like this: He was an old-time burglar whose pictures adorned many a rogue's gallery. Some twenty years of his life he had spent in prison here and there. He was a big, strong, courageous fellow with a hard face and a terrible tongue for swearing, especially at the sheriffs and their deputies, who seemed to be his natural enemies.

Dwight L. Moody was preaching in those days, and he went down to St. Louis one time to lead a union revival meeting. The *Globe Democrat* announced that it was going to print every word he said—his sermons, his prayers, and his exhortations. When Moody heard about this he made up his mind that he would read a lot of Scripture for the *Globe* to print, and that might count if his own poor words should fail. He did just that, and his sermons were sprinkled from day to day with Bible texts. The reporters tried their best to write original titles, and they put them in blazing headlines over the columns.

Now it so happened that Valentine Burke was in the St. Louis jail at that time awaiting trial. Solitary confinement was wearing on him, and he put in his time railing at the guards and reviling the sheriff on his daily visits.

One day somebody threw a *Globe Democrat* into his cell. The first thing that caught his eye was a big headline that read, "How the Jailer at Philippi Got Caught!" "Philippi?" he thought. "Oh, yes, that's up in Illinois. I've been there. I know that jailer, the old buzzard! Say, this is going to be good." So with a chuckle he sat down to read the story. But somehow the reading had a strange sound: "Paul and Silas, . . . a great earthquake." "What must I do to be saved?"

"How in the world has the *Globe Democrat* got to printing such stuff as this?" He looked at the date. Yes, it was Friday morning's paper, fresh from the press. He threw it down with an oath and walked around his cell like a caged lion. But by and by he picked up the paper again and read the sermon through. A restless fit grew on him. Again and again he picked up the paper and read the strange story. Something happened in that old burglar's heart that day. It cut him to the quick.

"What does it mean? Twenty years I've been a burglar and a thief, and I've never felt like this before. What can *I* do to be saved? I'm getting tired of this kind of life. If there is such a God as that preacher is telling about, I'll find out if it kills me to do it." Burke found out. Toward midnight, after long hours of bitter remorse for his wasted life and after many lonely and broken prayers, he became a changed man.

The next morning when the guard came around, Burke had a pleasant word for him. The guard eyed him with wonder. When the sheriff came, Burke greeted him in a friendly tone of voice and told him how he had found God at midnight in his cell after reading Moody's sermon. "Jim," said the sheriff to the guard, "You'd better keep an eye on Burke. He's playing the pious dodge on us, and he will be getting out of here his first chance."

In a few weeks Burke came to trial. Through some legal entanglement the case failed, and Burke was let loose. Friendless, an ex-burglar in a big city where he was known only as a criminal, Burke had a hard time for many months of heartache and sorrow. Not finding work in St. Louis, he went to New York, but he did not succeed there either. After six months he was back in St. Louis much discouraged. He did, however, hold fast to the God he had found at midnight in jail.

One day there came a message from the sheriff that he was wanted at the courthouse. Burke obeyed with a heavy heart. "Some old case that they've got against me I guess," he said to himself, "but if I'm guilty I'll tell them so. I'm done with lying."

The sheriff greeted him kindly. "Where have you been, Burke?"

"Oh, up in New York."

"What have you been doing there?"

"Trying to get a decent job," said Burke.

"Have you kept a good grip on that religion you told me about?"

"Yes," said Burke, "but I've had a hard time, sheriff. I haven't lost my religion, however."

It was then the tide turned. "Burke," said the sheriff, "I have had you shadowed every day that you were in New York. I suspected that your religion was a fraud, but I want to say to you that I know you've lived an honest Christian life. I have called you here to offer you the chief deputyship under me, and you can begin at once."

He was very faithful in his duties. Men everywhere learned to respect him. Years afterward the churches of St. Louis were ready for the coming of a great evangelist, who was to hold a meeting. Something happened, and he didn't come. The pastors were in trouble. Then one of them suggested that they send for Valentine Burke to tell his story. Burke led that meeting night after night, and many of the hard men of the city came to hear him. Many hearts were turned, as Burke's had been, from lives of crime and shame to Christian living.

When a man meets Jesus Christ, something happens. The transformation that takes place in the context of this relationship is one of life's greatest miracles. This is called conversion in our Christian vocabulary.

"But such an experience has never happened to me," says one. "I guess I haven't been converted." Since the experiences of some are so dramatic, the danger is to think of conversion only in terms of such unusual experiences. However, no two people have the same experience. That a change does take place when a man meets Jesus is clear. But the change differs in form with every different personality.

Let us look at three men who met Jesus while He was on earth.

Nathanael, a man who studied his Bible, looked for the coming Messiah. He went out to hear John the

Baptist preach. One day John introduced Jesus to the crowd, saying, "Behold the Lamb of God, which taketh away the sin of the world." As Nathanael looked Him over he was disappointed. "Could this be He?" He went away to pray. Many questions went through his mind. In the secret place there came into his heart a deep assurance that this was the long-looked-for Messiah.

Philip came and said, " 'We have found the one whom Moses wrote about in the book of the Law and whom the prophets also wrote about. He is Jesus son of Joseph, from Nazareth.' "

Nathanael's first response was, " 'Can anything good come from Nazareth?' . . .

" 'Come and see,' answered Philip.

"When Jesus saw Nathanael coming to him, he said about him, Here is a real Israelite; there is nothing false in him!'

"Nathanael asked him, 'How do you know me?'

"Jesus answered, 'I saw you when you were under the fig tree before Philip called you.'

" 'Teacher,' answered Nathanael, 'you are the Son of God! You are the King of Israel!' " (John 1:45-49, TEV).

Nathanael's childlike faith responded immediately. He had his doubts and prejudices, but these were quickly dispelled. When he met the Master it seemed a simple thing for him to accept Him. But not all are like Nathanael. I have met people who say, "I can't seem to believe as do others. I have an awful time with doubts and questions." For such, let us consider another man who met Jesus.

Take a look at this man Philip, who called Nathanael. Here was the real doubter among the twelve. We sometimes call Thomas "the doubter," and he was, but Philip was actually worse than he. You notice when he talked to Nathanael he called Jesus "son of Joseph," not "Son of God." In association with Jesus and the other disciples, again and again we find him expressing his doubts. It was Philip who emphasized the impossibility of feeding the five thousand. When certain Greeks came to see Jesus, Philip must have had some misgivings, for he didn't immediately introduce them. He went and talked it over with Andrew first. In John 14, where Jesus is talking about going back to His Father and how they should now know the Father because they knew Him, it was Philip who said, " 'Lord, show us the Father, and we shall be satisfied.' "

Philip was a "show me" man. He had a hard time believing. In due time, however, Philip became a teacher after the divine order. He knew whereof he spoke, and he taught with assurance that carried convictions to the hearers. The Divine Teacher was very patient with his unbelief because of his sincerity.

Do you find yourself filled with questions? To you Jesus says,"Ask, and you will receive"; and, "Come now, let us reason together." We need to ask the right questions before we can really understand the right answers. God does not give us a mind and then condemn us for using it. He promises to send the Spirit of truth to guide us, and He said, "Ye shall know the truth, and the truth shall make you free."

Perhaps you find yourself struggling, not so much with doubt and intellectual questions as with an evil temper, revenge, and the spirit of criticism. There is a man among the twelve just like you—John—who later became known as "the beloved." Here was a man who was not only proud, self-assertive, and ambitious for honor but impetuous and very resentful under injury.

He and his brother were called "sons of thunder."

On one occasion, when the people of Samaria didn't receive the Lord Jesus very courteously, these two men said, " 'Lord, do you want us to call fire down from heaven to destroy them?' " I'm sure you remember, too, the petition of their mother requesting that they might be permitted to occupy the highest positions of honor in the kingdom of God. On another occasion John said, "Master, we saw a man driving out demons in your name, and we told him to stop, because he doesn't belong to our group." John had thought that in checking this man he had in view the Lord's honor, but he soon began to see that he was jealous for his own.

Though by nature he had serious defects, John became distinguished as the "disciple whom Jesus loved." He was the one most always closest to Jesus. We see him on the Mount of Transfiguration. We see him in the Garden of Gethsemane. We see him braving the dangers of the judgment hall when everyone else had fled. We see him at the cross as Jesus places His mother in John's charge. He was one of the first to the tomb. Of him we read:

"In the life of the disciple John true sanctification is exemplified. During the years of his close association with Christ, he was often warned and cautioned by the Saviour; and these reproofs he accepted. As the character of the Divine One was manifested to him, John saw his own deficiencies, and was humbled by the revelation. Day by day, in contrast with his own violent spirit, he beheld the tenderness and forbearance of Jesus, and heard His lessons of humility and patience. Day by day his heart was drawn out to Christ, until he lost sight of self in love for his Master. The power and tenderness, the majesty and meekness, the strength and patience, that he saw in the daily life of the Son of God, filled his soul with admiration. He yielded his resentful, ambitious temper to the molding power of Christ, and divine love wrought in him a transformation of character" (*The Acts of the Apostles*, p. 557).

When you see Jesus as He really is, you see God as He really is, and you cannot help but admire and love Him. In fellowship with the Master you become more and more like Him, for by beholding we become changed. We become more and more like that to which we give our time and attention. Take time to make His acquaintance by reading more about Him and talking to Him more often, and you will be surprised what changes for good will be brought about in you.

Chapter 8

He Stumbled and Fell

Even if a man should be detected in some sin, my brothers, the spiritual ones among you should quietly set him back on the right path, not with any feeling of superiority but being yourselves on guard against temptation (Galatians 6:1, Phillips).

Let not thine heart be glad when he stumbleth (Proverbs 24:17).

If anyone does sin, we have someone who pleads with the Father on our behalf—Jesus Christ, the righteous one. And Christ himself is the means by which our sins are forgiven (1 John 2:1, 2, TEV).

Repent and believe the good news! (Mark 1:15, NIV).

Tom had been in the navy. He had worked side by side with rough men whose language was vulgar and profane. In fact, at the least provocation he himself could swear like a trooper. After an honorable discharge, Tom felt his need of an education and came to college. During the fall Week of Prayer he gave his heart to the Lord and decided to be a Christian. One afternoon shortly after his baptism everything seemed to go wrong. The machine in the shop where he worked suddenly balked. All at once there came from Tom's lips a series of words that shocked even himself. A deep sense of failure overwhelmed him. He stumbled and fell.

George had resolved never to smoke another cigarette. For several weeks he was successful, until one day an old friend that he had not seen for a long time dropped in to see him. In fact, they had been on many adventures together and had been old buddies for years. In the course of their conversation, as they relived some experiences, the friend reached into his shirt pocket, opened a pack of cigarettes, and handed one to George. Without thinking what he was doing, he took it. He had no more than lighted it and taken a few puffs when he realized what he had done. He stumbled and fell.

Jane always had a hard time telling it straight. She would lie, it seemed, even when it was to her advantage to tell the truth. They were always "white" lies, and exaggerations headed the list. She would tell harrowing experiences that really never happened just as she told them. Her insecurity made it necessary for her to "top" those of her friends in their chitchats of the evenings. In a Week of Devotion at college she began to see herself as she really was, and she made some important decisions. She would always tell the truth from then on. She wanted to be like Jesus.

One evening not long afterward, the girls were discussing the cost of dresses, each describing the best dress she ever had and the most expensive. Without thinking, Jane chimed in, telling about her best dress, and before she realized it she had the dress three times the original price and purchased at some fashionable department store, when in reality it was bought in a little hometown dress shop. She had not finished the last sentence when the sword of conscience pierced her through and through. While the girls never knew why she left so quickly, she went to her room and wept bitterly for failing again so soon.

She stumbled and fell.

Someone acquainted with these young people might have had a lot to say. For example, someone who had heard Tom swear that afternoon in the machine shop could have said, "I thought Tom was converted. So that's the kind of Christian he is—all sham and hypocrisy." Someone who had seen George smoking that cigarette that day might have said, "You know what? I saw George smoking today. I knew he couldn't hold out." And as for Jane, "I knew that she would never change." Isn't it strange that so many of us are so interested in watching others stumble and fall?

May I suggest that when we see someone stumble and fall we remember Galatians 6:1: "Even if a man should be detected in some sin, my brothers, the spiritual ones among you should quietly set him back on the right path, not with any feeling of superiority but being yourselves on guard against temptation" (Phillips). The New English Bible puts it, "Set him right again very gently."

Note the following by Ellen G. White:

"God wants us to help one another by a manifestation of sympathy and unselfish love. There are those who have inherited peculiar tempers and dispositions. They may be hard to deal with; but are we faultless? They are not to be discouraged. Their errors are not to be made common property. Christ pities and helps those who err in judgment. He has suffered death for every man, and because of this He has a touching and profound interest in every man.

"A man may be trying to serve God, but temptations from within and from without assail him. Satan and his angels urge and coax him to transgress. Perhaps he falls a prey to their temptings. How then do his brethren treat him? Do they speak harsh, cutting words, driving him further from the Saviour? What a sad sight for Christ and the angels to behold!

"Let us remember that we are struggling and falling, failing in speech and action to represent Christ, falling and rising again, despairing and hoping. Let us beware of dealing unkindly with those who, like ourselves, are subjects of temptation and who, like ourselves also, are the objects of Christ's unfailing love" (*Testimonies for the Church*, Vol. 9, p. 222).

At this point, for the sake of the Toms, Georges, and Janes—because there are so many of us like them—I would like to say, "I stumbled and fell. What do I do now?"

First, remember that to fall is not necessarily to fail. To lose a battle is not necessarily to lose the war. Notice the good news in 1 John 2:1, 2: "I am writing this to you, my children, so that you will not sin; but if anyone does sin, we have someone who pleads with the Father on our behalf—Jesus Christ, the righteous one. And Christ himself is the means by which our sins are forgiven" (TEV).

The redemptive attitude for one who has sinned is to repent. Over and over again the message of Jesus is to "repent and believe the good news" (Mark 1:15, NIV). The call to repentance was the message of prophets and apostles all through Scripture. It is for the sinner who first finds Christ as well as for the Christian who stumbles and falls.

What does it mean to repent? Why is repentance necessary? How does one experience it? Is it a once-and-for-all experience? I imagine for many people to repent means to be sorry and to shed bitter tears, an attitude of regret, remorse, and sadness. Of course, this is part of it. But if this is all it is, how can it be associated with good news? And how can one be sorry for something that he is glad he did? Suppose you had a good time last night that just thrilled you through and through. And suppose you tell me about it today and I should say, "Shame on you. Don't you know that that was a very sinful thing to do? If you ever expect to get to heaven you must be sorry for that. Come on, be sorry now!" Would you find tears of penitence rolling down your cheeks on the basis of that kind of counsel? I doubt it. While repentance may and does include tears, there is much more involved.

Repentance actually means "to have another mind." To experience repentance is to experience a change of mind and outlook, to see things in a different light. Phillips translates Mark 1:15 thus: "The time has come at last—the kingdom of God has arrived. You must change your hearts and minds and believe the good news." In Luke 13:5, "except you repent" he translates "unless your whole outlook is changed!" Repentance then involves getting your eyes open to the truth about things—the truth about God, the truth about ourselves, the truth about sin, the truth about the issues of life—and then doing something about it. This is why the apostle Paul was sent to the Gentiles—"to open their eyes, . . . that they . . . [might] receive forgiveness of sins" (Acts 26:18).

When we get our eyes open our attitudes change. This change of attitude is repentance. It is only as I see what I did last night in a new light that I can change my attitude toward it and really be sorry. If I discover that what I did keenly hurt someone I love very much, I can say, "Oh, man, I am sorry," and really mean it. If I discover that what I did last night set in operation a chain of circumstances or events that would destroy me in the end, you can understand how I would definitely regret it.

To further illustrate how attitudes change when we get our eyes open to the truth, I think of the experience of a friend of mine. As a newcomer to a certain community, he watched a black man in his garden across the street one afternoon. He was sitting on a box hoeing weeds. He would hoe a few, rest, hoe a few more, move the box up a bit, and repeat the process. My friend said to himself, "If that isn't the height of laziness!" He was prompted to say some unkind things about the neighbor.

Some time later he found out that that neighbor was an outstanding horticulturist. He had been in an automobile accident recently and had lost a leg. The stump had not had time to heal sufficiently to accept an artificial limb, but he loved his garden so much that he could not be kept out of it. He used the box to support himself, and being still weak from loss of blood, he needed to rest often.

When my friend got his eyes open to the truth about the man, his attitude toward him changed completely, and he was really sorry for the unkind things he had said about him. This is the way of repentance.

While repentance is characterized at times by sadness and sorrow over past mistakes, it is also accompanied by good judgment and wise moves in the right direction in the future. It is like this in every area of creative living. Truth steps up to a teenage hot-rod enthusiast and playboy and says, "Look, son, success as a lawyer, a doctor, a minister, an engineer, or what have you, depends on an education. It requires hard work and self-discipline, but it pays rich dividends and the joy of service and achievement. Repent, boy, and believe the good news. It is for you. Plan and work accordingly." If he gets his eyes open to these words of truth, if he awakens to the realization that one must deny himself present five-dollar pleasures for future fifty-dollar joys, he will repent. He will change his mind and his attitude and will do something about it.

In this light it is easy to see why repentance is necessary. Ezekiel tells us, "Repent, and turn yourselves from all your transgressions; so iniquity shall not be your ruin" (Ezekiel 18:30). Note Today's English Version of this passage: " 'Turn away from all the evil you are doing, and don't let your sin destroy you. Give up all the evil you have been doing, and get yourselves new minds and hearts. Why do you Israelites want to die? I do not want anyone to die,' says the Sovereign Lord. 'Turn away from your sins and live' " (Ezekiel 18:30-32).

The necessity for repenting is clearly evident in the fact that the direction in which we are going will lead to our ruin. The reason for repenting is not because an angry God will punish us in the judgment if we don't. It is the "goodness of God" that leads us to repentance (Romans 2:4). It is because a loving God wants to save us the natural consequences of wrong attitudes and actions.

Genuine repentance leads a person to confess his wrong without excusing it, to acknowledge his error without deception. Many confessions are only speeches of self-justification. "If this hadn't been true, and if that hadn't come about, and if it were not for this or that or the other circumstance, I never would have done what I did. Please forgive me." This is no confession. The redemptive attitude toward wrong is to admit it. Face the truth about it and about yourself. Face the truth about God and what is right. Give up false ideas and whatever hinders right actions and move forward.

True repentance is a gift of God (see Acts 5:30-32). This also is part of the Good News. One does not even need to repent before he comes to Christ. In fact, one must come to Christ before he can truly repent, because only in His perspective can he see things right. Note the following statement from the book *Steps to Christ*, page 26:

"Just here is a point on which many may err, and hence they fail of receiving the help that Christ desires to give them. They think that they cannot come to Christ unless they first repent, and that repentance prepares for the forgiveness of their sins. It is true that repentance does precede the forgiveness of sins; for it is only the broken and contrite heart that will feel the need of a Saviour. But must the sinner wait till he has repented before he can come to Jesus? Is repentance to be made an obstacle between the sinner and the Saviour? . . .

"We can no more repent without the Spirit of Christ to awaken the conscience than we can be pardoned without Christ" (p. 26).

The agent that effects this change in our minds and hearts is the Holy Spirit. He works in various ways. He is the Spirit of truth. He brings truth to us in His Word, through a friend, through providential circumstances of one kind or another, and through our consciences. He draws us to Himself, He enlightens us, He sets us free from the pride that would keep us from making the changes necessary, and He supplies the dynamics needed to accomplish the task.

Repentance, then, you see, is not a once-and-for-all experience. Nor is it a matter of sorrow for past sins alone. It is a continual process that deepens with every advance. Truth is always progressive. We grow in grace and in knowledge. The more we learn, the more we realize the sinfulness of sin, and the more we appreciate the goodness of God. At the same time "it is when we most fully comprehend the love of God that we best realize the sinfulness of sin" (*ibid.*, p. 36).

But what about this business of being converted? Were Tom, George, and Jane converted? If they were really and truly converted, would they have been spared the experience of stumbling and falling? How can I tell if I have been converted? Is it a once-and-for-all experience? When the minister said to me, "What you need, Paul, is to be converted," he explained to me that in conversion one becomes a new creature. Old things are passed away. All things become new. When I did not find myself a completely new creature, I figured I had not yet been converted. Was I correct in coming to this conclusion?

The word *conversion* means "change." For example, a convertible is a car that can be changed from a coupe to a roadster. In a spiritual sense it refers to the change that takes place when, under the influence of the Holy Spirit, one sees things in a new light (repents), and by the power of the Holy Spirit, does an about-face (changes direction). When this happens the person becomes a new creature. He is new, not in that he now has a new body, a new set of glands, or a new world in which to live, but new in that he has a new heart, a new outlook on life, a new goal. He is headed in a new direction, and he has a new dynamic in his life.

The Bible speaks of this change as being born again (see John 3). "As newborn babes, desire the sincere milk of the word, that ye may grow thereby" (1 Peter 2:2). The three young people described at the beginning of this chapter were all converted and were just beginning to grow. That they stumbled and fell does not mean they were not children of God. It does not mean they were not converted.

You see, conversion, like repentance, is not a once-and-for-all experience. One actually needs to be converted every day. "To follow Jesus requires wholehearted conversion at the start, and a repetition of this conversion every day" (Ellen G. White, in *The Seventh-day Adventist Bible Commentary*, Vol. 1, p. 1113). In writing to Brother and Sister C, Ellen G. White wrote, "You need a fresh conversion every day" (*Testimonies for the Church*, Vol. 1, p. 699). New insights bring new changes, and thus a Christian grows and becomes more and more mature. (See Chapter 10 on perfection.)

When Jesus told Peter that night that he would betray Him before morning, He also said, "But I have prayed for you, Simon, that your faith may not fail" (Luke 22:32, NIV). Was Jesus' prayer answered? Yes, it was. Peter fell, but he deeply repented of his fall, was converted afresh, and became a great preacher for God. He fell but did not fail. Notice, too, that Jesus said, "And when you have turned back [become converted] strengthen your brothers" (NIV). Peter learned a great deal that night, and it was a new beginning for him, even though he already had been following his Lord for some three years. His experience should be an encouragement to us.

Do you remember the caterpillar-butterfly illustration? When I realized that there were some things about the caterpillar life that still appealed to me, then concluded that I was not a butterfly yet—was not converted—I failed to see the difference between temptation and sin. Temptation is not sin. Jesus "was in all points tempted like as we are, yet without sin"

(Hebrews 4:15). Just because one is tempted does not mean he has sinned. Even to fall is not necessarily to fail.

Thus we see that both repentance and conversion are not once-and-for-all experiences, nor are they just duties we must perform or attitudes we must create in order to be saved. Both are part of the experiences offered us in fellowship with Jesus Christ, which are renewed every day. Repent and believe the Good News.

Chapter 9

"The Beauty of Holiness"

O worship the Lord in the beauty of holiness (Psalm 96:9).

Be ye holy; for I am holy (1 Peter 1:16).

Follow peace with all men, and holiness, without which no man shall see the Lord (Hebrews 12:14).

Right in the heart of Psalm 96—a psalm filled with song and praise, with joy and gladness and rejoicing—is the statement, "O worship the Lord in the beauty of holiness" (verse 9). For many, holiness is not associated with joy and gladness, but with gloom and sadness. In fact, too often there is associated with the term connotations that cause us to draw back, that frighten us or even discourage us. Some so-called holy men are very disgusting, even downright nauseating.

Peter admonishes, "Be holy in all that you do" (1 Peter 1:15, TEV). How can this be? Isaiah speaks of the people of God in this way: "And they shall call them, The holy people, The redeemed of the Lord" (Isaiah 62:12). How can we ever be such? In fact, in the song of Moses and the Lamb, the redeemed will sing, "Who shall not fear thee, O Lord, and glorify thy name? for thou only art holy" (Revelation 15:4). God alone is holy, how can we ever be? In spite of all this, David still speaks of "the beauty of holiness."

In describing the advantages or good qualities of a piece of equipment, you often hear the statement: "That is the beauty of it, it works so well, and it does so many things." There seems to be joy and satisfaction associated with it. Sometimes after hearing about something desirable, one may say, "Of course it it wonderful, but it is not for me; I can't afford it." And then another responds, "Oh, that's the beauty of it, it is available to all."

What is the beauty of holiness? I realize that some translations say, "Worship the Lord in holy array," but the image is clear. The people of God are invited to put on their beautiful garments, the white linen that represents the righteousness of Christ (see Revelation 19:8). While holiness cannot be compared with some material thing that can be purchased, there are ways in which one can speak of the beauty of it. In this sense of the word *beauty* I would like to look at holiness and show wherein lies its beauty.

First, let us define the term.

Philologists tell us that the words *healthy, hale, whole,* and *holy* all come from a single Anglo-Saxon root conveying the idea of wholeness and completeness. *Holiness* and *wholeness* have basically the same meaning. When Jesus said to the man at the pool of Bethesda, "Wilt thou be made whole?" He could have said, "Wilt thou be made holy?" Had He done so, I am sure He would have been misunderstood, for there were so many so-called holy men around that the man might have responded, "No, I don't want to be like them." But rightly understood, holiness is wholeness. Note a few significant statements from Ellen G. White:

"True holiness is wholeness in the service of God"

(*Christ's Object Lessons*, p. 48).

"Holiness is wholeness for God; it is the entire surrender of heart and life to the indwelling of the principles of heaven" (*The Desire of Ages*, p. 556).

"All righteous attributes of character dwell in God as a perfect, harmonious whole. Everyone who receives Christ as his personal Saviour is privileged to possess these attributes. This is the science of holiness" (*Testimonies for the Church*, Vol. 7, p. 276).

It is clear then that holiness is actually wholeness, completeness, perfect harmony, and entire fulfillment—complete agreement with God. Because "all righteous attributes of character dwell in God as a perfect, harmonious whole," you can see why God is holy.

With this concept of holiness in mind, let us note now wherein lies its beauty.

First of all, it is reasonable. The idea of wholeness—completeness—makes sense, doesn't it? Even a child is not satisfied with half a toy. If an automobile needs a valve job, new rings, new bearings, and a complete tune-up, is it not reasonable to take care of all these things, not just part of them? If you decide to thoroughly clean house, is it reasonable to do everything but wash the windows? Is not one's whole attention to a problem more effective than half-hearted consideration? Why go through life only half a person when you can be made whole by the Creator?

Surely the greatness of our God and His cause, as well as the importance of the work of redemption, demands wholehearted consecration. This is called our "reasonable service" (Romans 12:1). That is the beauty of holiness—wholeness. It is so reasonable.

Second, it is satisfying. True satisfaction comes from having all our needs met in a balanced way.

Wholeness, or holiness, provides a harmonious development of all the dimensions of man's being. The pseudosatisfactions of the world seem to meet temporarily a part of man's needs at the expense of others. In the long run this is frustrating, and it can be disastrous.

Some of life's greatest tragedies come from divided loyalties, indecision, and lack of complete commitment to a cause or a person. Halfhearted service is never really satisfying. An individual who is at civil war inside or who has never lost himself completely in a worthwhile endeavor does not really experience the joy of living. For life to be truly satisfying, there must be a magnificent obsession—something that calls forth the whole person of you in service for others. Holiness is wholeness for God, the complete commitment of self to Jesus Christ, and this makes for true self-realization.

The Greek and Hebrew words for holiness have the idea of separation in them. While holiness on God's part involves perfect harmony and supreme transcendence, our part involves separation from sin and complete dedication to and complete agreement with God. The separation called for on our part is only from those things that tend to destroy, compartmentalize, fragment, or divide and frustrate. There is no person so frustrated as the self-centered individual who resorts to pseudo means of satisfaction. The God-centered person is made whole. This brings true satisfaction.

Third, the beauty of holiness is that it is dynamic, creative, transforming in its results. Holiness is not just an ideal too high to reach. This could be very frustrating. Holiness is a condition achieved in a loving, trusting relationship with God, who provides the dynamic necessary to bring it about. You see, you ally yourself completely with the Source of power, wisdom, and love, and the Holy Spirit—the whole-making Spirit of God—takes over.

"Through faith the Holy Spirit works in the heart to create holiness therein; but this cannot be done unless the human agent will work with Christ. We can be fitted for heaven only through the work of the Holy Spirit upon the heart. . . . It is the work of the Holy Spirit to elevate the taste, to sanctify the heart, to ennoble the whole man" (*Selected Messages*, Book One, p. 374).

Holiness is not a goal too high to reach but an experience too meaningful to miss. Holiness is not something we must develop before we can have fellowship with God. It is rather a result of that fellowship. That is the beauty of it.

Fourth, it is so practical, so fitting, so suitable, so applicable to all of life's situations. Perhaps this idea crosses the mind of some: "How can one be all for God and religion when he has other interests and responsibilities? That may be all right for preachers who are paid to do this, but we have to make a living. How can we be all for God?

You remember that Peter said, "Be holy in all that you do" (1 Peter 1:15, TEV). Holiness is not something unrelated to life. It is life itself in harmony with the great source of life. In full agreement with Him, one is much better qualified to carry on his activities, interests, and responsibilities. That is why we are told in 1 Corinthians 10:31, "Whatsoever ye do, do all to the glory of God." There is no dichotomy here. There is not that complete separation between the natural and the supernatural. God's plan includes everything connected with human experience. When we are completely in harmony with our Creator, all the resources of heaven are at our disposal, and there is no limit to the possibilities of our development. Jesus said, "I am come that they might have life, and that they might have it more abundantly" (John 10:10). The holy life is the abundant life.

When one is wholly dedicated to God, it is true that his objectives and his sense of values will change as his vision broadens, but his interests and capabilities will increase. True holiness makes a man a better farmer, doctor, lawyer, teacher, minister, or whatever may be his legitimate vocation. That is the beauty of it.

Fifth, the beauty of holiness is that it is very rewarding both in this life and in the world to come. I shall discuss this in Chapter 15.

Finally, the beauty of holiness is that it is readily available and attainable. Someone may say, "All you have said about holiness sounds wonderful, but it is not for me. I can never be holy." The beauty of it *is* that it *is* for you. You *can be* holy. Jesus is saying to you today, "Wilt thou be made whole?" He doesn't ask you this question just to frustrate or ridicule you. He asks it because He loves you and wants you to share His holiness—His completeness. "He asks us to be absolutely and completely for Him in this world as He is for us in the presence of God" (*The Acts of the Apostles,* p. 566).

Enjoy the significance of this last statement. All Jesus asks of us is that we be absolutely and completely (wholly or holy) for Him as He is for us in heaven. When He says, "Be ye holy; for I am holy," He simply means "I'm all for you, Son. I'm all for you, Daughter. All I ask is that you be all for Me." Is that asking too much? Is that asking the impossible? By no means. This is something we can decide to do—to be all for Him.

As we contemplate the riches of holiness in fellowship with Jesus Christ, we "will come into possession of them" (see *ibid.*, p. 567). You see, then, what I mean when I say that holiness is not an ideal too high to reach but an experience too meaningful to miss. Don't be satisfied with anything less.

"Holiness is not rapture: it is an entire surrender of the will to God; it is living by every word that proceeds from the mouth of God; it is doing the will of our heavenly Father; it is trusting God in trial, in darkness as well as in the light; it is walking by faith and not by sight; it is relying on God with unquestioning confidence, and resting in His love" (*ibid.*, p. 51).

But, you say, what about this business of perfection? That subject we will consider in the next chapter.

Chapter 10

Perfect Righteousness

Be ye therefore perfect, even as your Father which is in heaven is perfect (Matthew 5:48).

Now the God of peace . . . make you perfect in every good work to do his will, working in you that which is wellpleasing in his sight, through Jesus Christ; to whom be glory for ever and ever. Amen (Hebrews 13:20, 21).

He shall be called, The Lord our Righteousness (Jeremiah 23:6).

Righteousness-by-faith says something like this: . . . "If you openly admit by your own mouth *that Jesus Christ is the Lord, and if you believe in* your own heart *that God raised him from the dead, you will be saved" (Romans 10:6-9, Phillips).*

Now my place is in him, and I am not dependent upon any of the self-achieved righteousness of the Law; God has given me that genuine righteousness which comes from faith in Christ (Philippians 3:9, Phillips).

What does it mean to be perfect? How many perfect people do you know? Must I be perfect before I die or before Jesus comes in order to be saved? Isn't perfection an impossibility as far as human nature is concerned?

Thinking along this line can be very discouraging when a person realizes the discrepancy between the ideal and the real—between what I ought to be and what I am. Some have been led to conclude: "I can never measure up to that standard, so why try?"

Actually there was on earth only one truly perfect man in the absolute sense, and that was Jesus. He was a man "in all points tempted like as we are, yet without sin" (Hebrews 4:15). He could say, "I do always those things that please him [the Father]" (John 8:29). He could also say, "He [Satan] has no power over me" (John 14:30, TEV). Such things cannot be said of you and me. "If we say that we have no sin, we deceive ourselves, and the truth is not in us" (1 John 1:8). If then I must be perfect as was Jesus, there would be no hope for me.

The Good News is that it is *His* perfect righteousness that makes possible our salvation. You see, it was the sin of one man—Adam—that brought us into this lost condition, and just so it is the righteousness of one man—Jesus—that saves us. This is why we read in Jeremiah 23:6 that Jesus will be known as "The Lord our Righteousness." Note what the apostle Paul says:

"Righteousness-by-faith says something like this: . . . 'If you openly admit by *your own mouth* that Jesus Christ is the Lord, and if you believe in *your own heart* that God raised him from the dead, you will be saved' " (Romans 10:6-9, Phillips).

"It is true that through the sin of one man death began to rule because of that one man. But how much greater is the result of what was done by the one man, Jesus Christ! . . . And just as all people were made sinners as the result of the disobedience of one man, in the same way they will all be put right with God as the result of the obedience of the one man" (Romans 5:17-19, TEV).

But, must we not also be righteous? Oh, yes. Our righteousness is possible, however, only in Him, and it comes about by faith. How is this? First of all, God puts people completely right with Himself through faith in Jesus: "God puts people right through their faith in Jesus Christ" (Romans 3:22, TEV).

Having put them right, He then proceeds to make them right. "The atonement of Christ is not a mere skillful way to have our sins pardoned; it is a divine remedy for the cure of transgression and the restoration of spiritual health" (*Seventh-day Adventist Bible Commentary*, Vol. 6, p. 1074).

How does He do this? "The only way in which he could set and keep men right was to make himself visible and familiar to their eyes" (*Signs of the Times*, January 20, 1890). We are influenced by the company we keep, and we become more and more like that which we behold. The more we walk and talk with Jesus, the more we cultivate the consciousness of His presence, the more we become like Him. When we see what a wonderful person He is and realize that He is the express image of His Father so that God is like that, too, we know we can trust Him to fulfill His promises. If we trust Jesus enough to do whatever He says and to follow wherever He leads, we can know that he who has begun a good work in us will finish it (see Philippians 1:6). This trust we call *faith*.

Now you may say, "I guess I just don't have enough faith." Faith is not some mystical power you must muster up or pray down. It is not something you and I must accomplish in order for God to make us righteous. Faith is not the result of our accomplishments. It comes naturally when we behold God's accomplishments. That is why we read, "Faith cometh by hearing, and hearing by the word of God" (Romans 10:17). The more we learn about Him as revealed in Jesus, the more our faith in Him grows.

It is like having faith in a surgeon. Suppose you

were an eye surgeon, and I needed your services. In order for you to help me, I must have utmost confidence or faith in you. I must trust you enough to let you put me to sleep and do to me whatever you please. Now, is my faith in you dependent upon *my* accomplishments? By no means. My faith in you is dependent upon *your* accomplishments. I will find out all I can about you. Where did you take your training? Have you ever done this procedure before, and how did it come out? Are you the kind of person who cares for his patients? Are you a man of integrity? Then if I am convinced you are trustworthy, I will put myself in your hands. And if you are to help me, I must be willing to follow your instructions explicitly.

So it is with our faith in Jesus. It is based on His accomplishments, not ours. As I find that He is trustworthy, I put myself in His hands.

But what about being perfect? Perfection as applied to man is not arriving at a static state beyond which there is no room for improvement. It is becoming. It is growing or maturing. It is forgetting the past and pressing forward to the goal of Christlikeness. Paul tells us: "I do not consider myself to have 'arrived,' spiritually, nor do I consider myself already perfect. . . . But I do concentrate on this: I leave the past behind and with hands outstretched to whatever lies ahead I go straight for the goal—my reward the honor of my high calling by God in Christ Jesus. All of us who are spiritually adult should set ourselves this sort of ambition" (Philippians 3:12-15, Phillips).

Perfection, then, is not "arriving," but making constant improvement. "It is your work to advance toward perfection, making constant improvement, until at last you are pronounced worthy to receive immortal life. And even then the work of progression will not cease, but *will continue throughout eternity*" (Ellen G. White, *In Heavenly Places,* p. 186, italics supplied). And "at every stage of development our life may be perfect; yet if God's purpose for us is fulfilled, there will be *continual advancement*" (*Christ's Object Lessons,* p. 65, italics supplied).

There are two ways in which we can be perfect *now* and still have a long way to go. First of all, we can know perfect forgiveness. Notice the present tense in the following statement: "While we cannot claim perfection of the flesh, we may have Christian perfection of the soul. Through the sacrifice made in our behalf, sins may be perfectly forgiven" (*Selected Messages,* Book Two, p. 32). Second, we may know a perfect love relationship with our heavenly Father in the context of which we can grow. In the same reference quoted above, we read, "We may enjoy the favor of God." Note again the present tense.

Here is a little boy who is just learning to walk. Naturally he stumbles and falls many times. What would you think of his father if he would say to his son, "Look, Junior, you can't even take two steps without falling down. What kind of a boy are you anyway? If you can't do better than that, you are not my son. When you can learn to walk without stumbling, I'll be your father and you will be my son." Or here is a teenager who makes some foolish decision and gets into trouble. What would you think of the father if he said, "Well, Son, that was a crazy thing to do. You certainly didn't use good judgment that time. Listen, boy, until you get some sense into that head of yours, you're not my son, and I am not your father. Don't expect me to get you out of trouble." I'm sure you question the judgment of these fathers.

A mature father will understand that in a loving

relationship with him little Junior will learn to walk, and the teenage son, in fellowship with an understanding, loving father, will learn to exercise better judgment as he grows and develops. "If you then, though you are evil, know how to give good gifts to your children, how much more will your Father in heaven give the Holy Spirit to those who ask him!" (Luke 11:13, NIV).

Too often when we hear sermons or read about Christ, our righteousness, we focus on ourselves to determine how like Christ we are becoming, and seeing how far short we come, we get discouraged. The focus should be not on our imperfect lives but on Jesus and His perfect life. "Turn to me and be saved, all you ends of the earth; for I am God, and there is no other. . . . 'In the Lord alone are righteousness and strength' " (Isaiah 45:22-24, NIV).

"You are not to look to yourself, not to let the mind dwell upon self, but look to Christ. Let the mind dwell upon His love, upon the beauty, the perfection, of His character. Christ in His self-denial, Christ in His humiliation, Christ in His purity and holiness, Christ in His matchless love—this is the subject for the soul's contemplation. It is by loving Him, copying Him, depending wholly upon Him, that you are to be transformed into His likeness" (*Steps to Christ*, pp. 70, 71).

Turn your eyes upon Jesus,
    Look full in His wonderful face,
And the things of earth will grow strangely dim
    In the light of His glory and grace.
—Helen H. Lemmel.*

Chapter 11

The Judgment

God shall bring every work into judgment, with every secret thing, whether it be good, or whether it be evil (Ecclesiastes 12:14).

The hour of his judgment is come (Revelation 14:7).

Love is made complete among us so that we will have confidence on the day of judgment. . . . There is no fear in love. But perfect love drives out fear (1 John 4:17, 18, NIV).

She was only ten years old, but she had a very sensitive conscience, and she took spiritual things seriously. She generally went to bed around 8:30 PM on school nights and was soon fast asleep. One night, however, as her father passed by her bedroom door on his way to bed, he heard her sobbing as if her heart would break. It was close to ten o'clock by that time. He went into her room and asked, "What in the world is the matter, honey? What is wrong?"

That day in church school the teacher in her Bible class had emphasized the importance of confessing our sins and making everything right with God and our fellowmen. The teacher pointed out that the confession must be specific. It was not enough just to say, "Dear Jesus, please forgive all my sins. Thank You," then jump into bed thinking all had been taken care of. Oh, no; one must confess each sin committed separately. And then it was indelibly impressed upon the little girl's mind that one unconfessed sin on the record book would keep a person out of heaven. After telling about the lesson, she said through her tears, "But, Daddy, what if I have forgotten one?"

Have you ever wondered about that? Has the thought of your name's coming up in the judgment ever filled your heart with fear? Some Christians I know seem to feel that way. Some think that when God forgives sins, He does so provisionally. They think He still keeps them on the record and holds them against the individuals until the end, so that in case we don't make it, He will punish us for all the sins we have ever committed. What a picture of God! What a concept of our heavenly Father! No wonder some hearts are filled with fear when the judgment is mentioned.

God is a God of judgment, but that is not because He is a despot or a tyrant but because He always uses good judgment in all that He does. You would not want Him to be otherwise. Love demands justice. When you understand the great controversy between Christ and Satan, you realize that there needs to be a judgment in the end to clarify the issues and the character of all involved. The judgment is for the purpose of acquitting the innocent as well as condemning the guilty. On such an occasion it is important that the whole picture be seen with all details in true perspective. God has made provision for this by keeping a record of everything, including the motives behind every action.

Since God has been misrepresented by Satan, it must be demonstrated that God's judgments are just. If you and I are to be made permanent citizens of the earth made new, it must be clearly seen that we are safe to save—safe to be welcomed into the family of God for eternity. The inhabitants of the unfallen worlds as well as the angels of heaven do not want sin to rise again. Neither do we. The great day of judgment is appointed to accomplish all this.

Now in order for me to have a fair trial, all the facts of my life must be included. That is why a complete record is kept. That is why, even though God has forgiven my sins, the record remains. Not that God will hold it against me if I fail in the end but that it may be seen how I came to be what I am.

You see, what a person is, is more important than what a person does. When probation closes, the decree goes forth, "He that is, . . . let him be" (Revelation 22:11). In the judgment it will be seen how he came so to be. Thus the records are there, not to be held against us but there *for* us. A God of love wants me to know why I can't be admitted to heaven. He also wants it made clear in the minds of friends of mine who will miss me and wonder why I am not there, if that is the case. Should anyone question the judgment of God in any instance, the records are there to prove His love and justice. Incidentally, that is what the millennium is for. During that thousand-year period, time will be given to settle all such questions in the minds of the redeemed. At the end of the millennium it will be made plain to all, including the wicked, that Satan's accusations against God are false and that all His judgments are right. All will exclaim, " 'True and righteous are thy judgments.' 'Just and true are thy ways, thou King of saints.' " Then, "every knee shall bow, . . . and every tongue shall confess" that Jesus Christ is Lord to the glory of God.

Will one unconfessed sin on the record keep me

out? Yes, but not because it is on the record and I have forgotten to confess it. It will be because it is in my heart, and I refused to give it up. One unconfessed sin *cherished* will unfit me for life eternal (see *Steps to Christ*, p. 34).

When you realize that in the judgment, the Presiding Judge is your heavenly Father, who loves you very much; the Attorney who pleads your case is your Elder Brother, who gave His life for you and who has never lost a case; the Holy Spirit and the angels of heaven are your witnesses; and all heaven is in your favor—you have nothing to fear. Only Satan is your accuser, and he has no chance to win his case against you. Thus confidence and assurance can be yours: "We will have confidence on the day of judgment" (1 John 4:17, NIV). In Chapter 14 these thoughts are developed further.

Chapter 12

Why Pray?

Then Jesus told his disciples a parable to teach them that they should always pray and never become discouraged. "In a certain town there was a judge who neither feared God nor respected man. And there was a widow in that same town who kept coming to him and pleading for her rights, saying, 'Help me against my opponent!' For a long time the judge refused to act, but at last he said to himself, 'Even though I don't fear God or respect man, yet because of all the trouble this widow is giving me, I will see to it that she gets her rights. If I don't, she will keep on coming and finally wear me out!' "

And the Lord continued, "Listen to what that corrupt judge said. Now, will God not judge in favor of his own people who cry to him day and night for help? Will he be slow to help them? I tell you, he will judge in their favor and do it quickly. But will the Son of Man find faith on earth when he comes?" (Luke 18:1-8, TEV).

Why tell God what He already knows?

Will God upset the laws of nature just for me?

How can God answer conflicting prayers?

Have you ever experienced a real answer to prayer? I am sure you have heard or read many stories of those who have, if you can't put your finger on one of your own.

Perhaps you recall some of Josephine Cunnington

Edwards' experiences. While they were working their way through college, her husband needed some new shirts. She prayed, and someone brought four shirts just her husband's size. On another occasion the children were the only ones on the block without tricycles. She prayed about this, too, and a day or so later two tricycles were brought for the children.

On one occasion in the mission field she lost her scissors. Needing them badly, she prayed. The next day a pair of scissors came in the mail from a good man in Minneapolis, Minnesota. He said in a letter, "I don't know why I am sending you these. I just have a feeling you need them." And they were better scissors than the ones she had lost. The strange part of it all was that the man in Minneapolis mailed the parcel eight weeks earlier, perhaps even before she had lost the scissors.

But what about people who pray, and nothing happens? Constance Foster wrote in *Guideposts* magazine of a young college girl who was failing to make passing grades in certain subjects and was warned that she would be dropped at the end of the year. She prayed earnestly for success but nevertheless failed her examinations. The college dropped her, and she thought that her prayer was not answered.

A few weeks later she took some tests and discovered that she had unusual gifts in spatial perception and mechanical ability. With some encouragement she took a technical course in X-ray therapy and medical techniques. Today, as head of a large hospital laboratory with a dozen assistants under her direction, she is making a splendid salary and is happy in her work.

God did answer her prayers, though at first it seemed as if nothing happened. Often our plans fail that God's plans for us might succeed. Not always, of course, because sometimes we fail on account of not working or thinking hard enough.

In this technical age—this skeptical age—of ours there are always questions which come into our minds.

Why pray? Must we inform God about our needs? Does He not know all about us?

Will God upset the laws of nature just to answer your prayers and mine?

Can we change God's mind? Does He not say, "I am God and I change not?"

How can God answer conflicting prayers? I pray for rain. My neighbor prays for it not to rain. How can both be answered?

Unless prayer is grounded upon a sound structure of belief, it becomes like letters to Santa Claus, mere wishful thinking, or at best, just a form of therapeutic thinking or meditation. Let us consider a number of basic beliefs upon which a meaningful prayer experience must be built.

No. 1. God is a personal being—a God of love—with whom we can communicate. He is present in this world, and He cares about us and desires to help us. He knows what is best for our lives, and He makes every provision for our welfare. Being a God of love, He is interested in our response to His love, and our communication with Him is meaningful to Him as in any love relationship.

No. 2. Man is a being capable of loving and responding to love. He is a free being—a free moral agent. This is the only kind of being a God of love would create. This kind alone would satisfy His heart of love, for He is not interested in the love of a puppet, a robot, or an automaton any more than we are.

No. 3. The universe is both faithful and flexible to God and man. This is constantly being verified in the laboratories today. No other kind of universe could provide security or be an acceptable abode for man. The miracles of Jesus clearly indicate that the Creator is in perfect control of the forces of nature.

No. 4. We are in the midst of a great controversy. A war is on between good and evil. Relationships in time of war are somewhat different from those in times of peace. There are some things we cannot do in times of war that we can do in times of peace. In the light of this great controversy, not everything that happens is God's will, but nothing can happen to defeat His will. His plans may be thwarted, but His victory is certain. And in this controversy it is not what happens to us but how we react to what happens that determines our relationships.

Now, when we consider prayer in the light of these four basic premises and in the context of an ideal love relationship, we are better prepared to answer some of the questions asked. The question, "Why pray?" is the same as to ask, "Why communicate?" Prayer is communication with God as with a loved one or friend. In any love relation, communication is necessary. Prayer is not merely asking God for things but talking to God about things.

Perhaps you have heard the statement, "God always answers prayer. He either says yes or no or wait awhile." Now, while this is true, it implies that prayer is only a matter of requests to be granted, denied, or postponed. In the light of a love relationship there are thousands of prayers that do not need answering. We merely want to share our joys and our sorrows. We even enjoy communication in silence. This is what prayer is to the Christian who understands God.

Should we inform God about what He knows already? Of course we should. Just as parents love to have their children come to them with needs and requests already known to them, so our heavenly Father longs for the same from us.

Will God upset the laws of nature just because we pray? The forces of nature are God's servants. He uses them to accomplish His purposes. We said that the universe is both faithful and flexible. Faithful in the sense that the laws of nature are consistent and dependable, because God is. Flexible in that they are always under His perfect control. There is no upsetting of the law or violation of natural principles if God should choose to speed up some process or temporarily suspend a particular force because of the demands of a higher law—the law of life and love. This is entirely consistent with the character of God as revealed by Jesus and with the character of the universe as discovered by scientists in the field and in the laboratory.

Miracles are not out of harmony with natural law. In fact, everything God does is in perfect harmony with His law, which is a transcript of His character. These principles are written in the very nature of the universe.

How can God answer conflicting prayers? This in no way puts Him in a dilemma. He can see the basic needs behind each petition, and He has a thousand ways of supplying these. God can answer the prayers of both of the men who are concerned about rain by meeting the needs of each, rain or no rain. God is more interested in our growth and character development than in our passing wishes or desires.

Someone has said:

> Many of us lose confidence in prayer because we

do not realize the answer.

We ask for strength, and God gives difficulties which make us strong.

We pray for wisdom, and God sends us problems, the solution of which develops wisdom.

We plead for prosperity, and God give us brain and brawn to work.

We cry for courage, and God gives us dangers to overcome.

We ask for favors, and God gives us opportunities.

When we pray for showers of blessing, God often sends us clouds.

Before us, even as behind, God is, and all is well.

In the story of the corrupt judge in the New Testament, the widow kept on pleading until finally her request was granted. How does this apply? Is God finally persuaded by our constant repetition? Will He eventually get tired of our pestering Him and grant our requests? Will He most likely answer those who perseveringly present their requests in the most persuasive language? Is Jesus comparing our heavenly Father with the unjust judge?

By no means. He is teaching by contrast rather than by comparison. If a corrupt judge, simply because the petitioner becomes a nuisance, will finally grant a request, how much more shall a loving heavenly Father, because of His deep concern for us, hear and answer us.

Jesus is saying that men ought always to pray and not to faint, because He knows our weaknesses. He knows, too, that only as we keep in touch with Him can we be spared the overwhelming power of the evil one. Only as we continue to commune with God will our perspective be kept clear and our sense of values sound. That is why He says, "Keep asking." "There is no danger that the Lord will neglect the prayers of His people. The danger is that in temptation and trial they will become discouraged, and fail to persevere in prayer" (*Christ's Object Lessons*, p. 175).

It is in the setting of the time of the end that our Lord gave the parable. No wonder He says, "Be on watch and pray always that you will have the strength to go safely through all those things that will happen and to stand before the Son of Man" (Luke 21:36, TEV).

Isn't it strange that so great a privilege as prayer—communion with our Creator—is so little understood, appreciated, and practiced?

Again and again in Scripture we are admonished to pray. God's great men down through the ages were men of prayer. We are told that Jesus spent whole nights in prayer and that this was the secret of His power. The apostle Paul was a man of prayer. He counseled the Thessalonians to "pray without ceasing" (1 Thessalonians 5:17).

How can one pray without ceasing? Or how can one pray even for one full night? What would you say to God after the first fifteen minutes? Even if you mentioned all your problems and all of everyone else's problems you knew about, all the missionaries, the colporteurs, and everything else you could think of that might be worth praying about, I doubt that it would take half the night.

These questions imply that prayer consists only of talking to God. True prayer is not a one-way matter. If you understand that prayer includes not only talking to God but listening to what He has to say in His Word and by His Spirit, then you can see how time could pass quickly in wrestling with problems of great importance. To pray without ceasing means to be constantly in an attitude of communion with God as those who walk with God.

Chapter 13

The Prayer Of Faith

Ask and it will be given to you (Matthew 7:7, Phillips).

But he must ask in sincere faith without secret doubts as to whether he really wants God's help or not. The man who trusts God, but with inward reservations, is like a wave of the sea, carried forward by the wind one moment and driven back the next. That sort of man cannot hope to receive anything from the Lord, and the life of a man of divided loyalty will reveal instability at every turn (James 1:6-8, Phillips).

"Mrs. Fisher, if you had had more faith, your son would be alive today." The spokesman was a well-meaning, sincere little Christian woman who didn't quite understand. You see, Dr. Oral Fisher, an outstanding young Christian dentist with a bright future, found out that he had cancer. He and his family prayed much about this, and in harmony with the instruction in the Book of James they called for the elders of the church to anoint him with oil in the name of the Lord and to pray for his healing. This we were glad to do. But for some reason, the Lord did not see fit to heal him. He died. Then it was that the well-meaning statement was made. As a result, in addition to the burden of grief from losing her only son, Mrs. Fisher had the added load of guilt.

What is a prayer of faith? Does getting an answer

depend upon how much faith I can muster? If I pray and get no answer, does this mean I have no faith? And if I pray and something miraculous happens, does this indicate that I have great faith? If so, how does it happen that miraculous answers have at times come after the person has lost faith?

I once read of an elderly widow named Mrs. Horton, whose husband's death had left her almost destitute. She was in danger of losing her large home. She could no longer meet the heavy expense of maintaining it. Mrs. Horton asked her minister to pray that she might by some miracle be able to keep it, together with all of her cherished possessions. A few months later she wrote to her minister, "We both prayed, but nothing happened." The house was sold at auction the following week, and Mrs. Horton was heartbroken.

During the next few days Mrs. Horton went through her house with tear-stained eyes, sorting and discarding the accumulation from long years of living there. In the attic she ran across an old stamp collection that had been in her husband's family for years. She almost threw it out as rubbish. But somehow, something made her save it. A year went by before she thought of it again. The house had been sold. She was bitter. Her prayer had not been answered. Then one day she happened to see in a large city newspaper a list of the values of certain rare stamps. She took the old collection to the dealer, and when she left his office, she was dazed, for in her purse she had his check for nearly $11,000.

The big house had been much too large for an older woman to care for comfortably. She did not need all that space. Today she realizes that what she required was smaller living quarters and enough money in the bank for expenses. This was exactly what God gave her in answer to her supposedly unanswered prayer.

How much must one believe to get the right answers?

Some years ago while I was pastor of the Walla Walla College Church, one of the members of my congregation, a very lovely Christian woman, found that she had inoperable cancer. She, too, called for the elders of the church to come and pray for her and anoint her with oil in the name of the Lord. As we were talking with her, in preparation for the anointing, she said, "Elder Heubach, one thing disturbs me: I know that our prayers can be answered only if we believe. Jesus said again and again, 'according to your faith be it unto you.' I'm afraid I don't have enough faith. Oh, yes, I believe God could answer our prayer. I don't question the fact that He could heal me. God can do anything. But somehow I can't believe that He *will* heal me. Let me tell you why. My mother had cancer. They prayed for her. She died. Several other relatives went through the same experience. How can I believe He will heal me? Maybe you don't want to go ahead with this service."

What would you have said to her? When we learn to know God as revealed in Jesus Christ, we gradually come to trust Him and not our prayer. In the prayer of faith we trust God, not our ideas for God. I could tell our dear little lady in Walla Walla, "You don't need to believe He will heal you. Just believe that He loves you and that He will be with you always and will do whatever is best for you under all circumstances."

"Do you mean to say that it is not necessary for me to believe that He will heal me?"

"That is right. Leave that with Him. We can ask Him to heal you, and we will, but let us allow Him to decide what to do," I replied.

She breathed a great sigh of relief. As a result of our conversation and our prayer together, she gained a new concept of God's love and the meaning of faith. Whereas the physician gave her only a few months to live, the Lord gave her five wonderful years. She finally did succumb to cancer, but it was with a strong faith in God that she went to her rest.

The prayer of faith, then, is a prayer of intelligent commitment to God. It is a prayer of sharing our heart's desires in perfect confidence. It involves cultivating constantly the consciousness of God's presence. It involves knowing God so well and trusting Him so completely that we will do anything He asks us to do. We will adopt the counsel of the wise man, which says, "Trust in the Lord with all thine heart; and lean not unto thine own understanding. In all thy ways acknowledge him, and he shall direct thy paths" (Proverbs 3:5, 6). We will trust Him and not our ideas of Him.

How shall we pray for God's guidance? How can we discover His will for us in making important decisions? Shall we ask for signs if when we pray we get no answers? Suppose I am faced with two alternatives, two opportunities, two calls to service, both legitimate. I must make a decision. Shall I pray, "Lord, here is job A, and here is job B? If by noon tomorrow so and so happens, I'll know You want me to take A. If it doesn't happen, then I'll know Your will for me is B."

What am I doing when I set up a situation like this? Am I not virtually saying, "Lord, apparently You don't want to talk to me, so I'll set You up a signal system. I need to know right now. If You are interested in me, You will help me." Am I not also asking God to make my decision for me so I can blame Him if it doesn't work out right? And again, am I not forcing His hand by virtually saying, "Look, Lord, I must know by noon tomorrow, so I'm going to put You on the spot. No matter which way it turns out, I will have Your answer. Be sure You see that it comes out right."

There are many reasons why He might not want me to know by tomorrow. Is He going to be pressured into answering by a trick like that? By no means.

"Every human being, created in the image of God, is endowed with a power akin to that of the Creator—individuality, power to think and to do" (*Education*, p. 17). God wants men in whom this power is developed. He does not want robots, puppets, or automatons to serve Him. If He made all our decisions for us, that is just what we would be. Let us not ask Him to make our decisions for us. Let us rather ask Him to give us good sense, good judgment, help in understanding the issues that are involved, and courage and strength to do what is right.

God has promised to guide us. If there seems to be no immediate indication of His will, keep trusting and praying. He may either close one door and open another so that it will be very plain which way to go, or else He may say, "I'm leaving it up to you. You decide. I will bless you whichever way you take. If you make mistakes, I will help you learn from them." I don't believe God is the kind of God who says, "You had better do My will, or else." And then I say, "All right, Lord, I really want to. What do you want me to do?" And He replies, "Never mind, but you had better do it." God does not treat us in this way.

God is more interested in what I *am* than what I *do*. More important than external signs for me is good judgment developed under the guidance of the Holy Spirit through the Written Word. Therefore God leaves some things up to me, that I may learn by experience.

The prayer of faith, then, is a prayer for insight, for good judgment, for ability, and for strength to act in harmony with what we do understand. That is why we must continually study His Word to keep our spiritual vision clear.

Too often our prayers are entirely self-centered. We seem to think only of *our* needs, *our* interests, *our* desires, and *our* doings. The more closely we become associated with Jesus, the more we become like Him. We are told that "from His earliest years He was possessed of one purpose; He lived to bless others" (*The Desire of Ages*, p. 70). More and more the burden of our prayers will be concerned with Him and others. Increasingly we will see that persons are more important than things and that we need to be more loving and kind. To have a clear mind and an understanding heart so that we can be a greater blessing to others will dominate our prayers.

One reason why our prayers are so self-centered is because of our insecurity. The prayer of faith is the prayer rooted in complete trust in God. This gives us a security that enables us to give more thought to concern for others, and this makes for increasing spiritual maturity.

Chapter 14

Can I Be Sure Of Life Eternal?

Of this I am convinced, that He who has begun a good work in you will bring it to completion until the day of Christ Jesus (Philippians 1:6, Berkeley).

To this hope we anchor the soul safely and securely and it reaches on into the Holy of Holies, where Jesus entered in for us in advance (Hebrews 6:19, 20, Berkeley).

What if, after I have denied myself all the pleasures of this life in order to gain the life hereafter, I should lose out at the last minute and not make it? I will have had neither the joy of this life nor the privilege of enjoying the next. Why not be sure of this one at least? It seems a risky business to stake all you've got on something so far in the future and not too tangible at that; especially when the odds are against you.

Have you ever thought like that? Can a person be sure of life eternal? This is surely a reasonable question, for the insecurity that comes from uncertainty is not conducive to peace of mind. If any promises in God's Word are clear and specific, those regarding peace of mind are definitely so. Note a few: "Great peace have they which love thy law: and nothing shall offend them" (Psalm 119:165). "Thou wilt keep him in perfect peace, whose mind is stayed on thee: because he trusteth in thee" (Isaiah 26:3). "Peace I leave with you, my peace I give unto you: not as the world giveth, give I unto you. Let not your heart be troubled, neither let it be afraid" (John 14:27).

Some seem to have the feeling that God is looking for every excuse He can find to keep us out of the kingdom. Others seem to think that only a select few—the elect—will make it, and that there is just no hope for the rest of us who have too hard a time doing what is right.

Many take a fatalistic attitude and say that we are predestined to be saved or lost, and there is nothing we can do about it. Among some Christians this takes a very subtle form: God knows the end from the beginning, and so He knows whether I will be saved or lost. If He knows that I will be lost, then that is all I can expect.

Does the Bible teach predestination? Yes, it does. To misunderstand it can be very discouraging. When you understand it correctly, it is very satisfying and assuring, giving one a security that surpasses anything the world has to offer. Note some statements from Ephesians 1: ". . . according as he hath chosen us in him before the foundation of the world" (verse 4). ". . . having predestinated us unto the adoption of children by Jesus Christ to himself, according to the good pleasure of his will" (verse 5). "In whom also we have obtained an inheritance, being predestinated according to the purpose of him who worketh all things after the counsel of his own will" (verse 11).

From these statements it would seem to the superficial observer that before the foundation of the world it was already decided who would be saved—predetermined by God, who works all things according to His own will. Is that it?

To begin with, let us establish two important truths: First, we are free moral agents. This the Bible clearly teaches. "Choose you this day whom ye will serve" (Joshua 24:15). "Whosoever will, let him take the water of life freely" (Revelation 22:17). "I have set before you life and death, blessing and cursing: therefore choose life, that both thou and thy seed may live" (Deuteronomy 30:19). If our destiny is predetermined, these texts are not true—we have no choice.

Second, no one is predestined to be lost: "The Lord is . . . not willing that any should perish, but that all should come to repentance" (2 Peter 3:9). "Who will have all men to be saved, and to come unto the knowledge of the truth" (1 Timothy 2:4). "Say unto them, As I live, saith the Lord God, I have no pleasure in the death of the wicked; but that the wicked turn from his way and live: turn ye, turn ye from your evil ways; for why will ye die, O house of Israel?" (Ezekiel 33:11). This last text would be the height of mockery if they were predestined by God to be lost.

What, then, is predetermined? Simply this: "The wages of sin is death, but the free gift of God is eternal life in Christ Jesus our Lord" (Romans 6:23, RSV). This was determined before God created the earth. This is not arbitrary on God's part. In the very nature of the laws of life it necessarily follows that if one cuts himself off from the Source of life, he dies. Note another text: "As in Adam all die, even so in Christ shall all be made alive" (1 Corinthians 15:22). That is, all who choose to believe Satan rather than God, as did Adam, will naturally suffer the consequences. However, all who choose to believe in Christ shall be made alive. And this is what was decided before the creation of the world. The plan of salvation was not an afterthought.

Notice that in both Romans and First Corinthians the key words are "in Christ." Go back now and read Ephesians 1 and observe how many times the words "in Christ" are used. All the promised blessings are to be realized "in Christ." The statement that God "worketh all things after the counsel of his own will" is reassuring. We serve the God who is able to carry out His plans. He purposes to save all who accept Jesus Christ. Of this we can be sure.

But what about the "elect"? Who are they? Can I be among them? Or are these a chosen few? The Bible tells us that "Israel" is God's "elect" (Isaiah 45:4). They were chosen of God to be His witnesses in the earth. Since they failed to accomplish their mission, God has chosen the Christian church to do the job. "They are not all Israel, which are of Israel. . . . They which are the children of the flesh, these are not the children of God: but the children of the promise are counted for the seed" (Romans 9:6-8). "And if ye be Christ's, then are ye Abraham's seed, and heirs according to the promise" (Galatians 3:29). So who are the elect? Israel—spiritual Israel. Can I be among them? Yes, I can. How? By being Christ's. "If ye be Christ's," then you are one of the elect of God. There is no doubt about it. You can be sure of life eternal "in Christ."

In Romans 8:30 we read, "Moreover whom he did predestinate, them he also called." Have you ever felt the call of God by His Holy Spirit in your own heart? If you answer that call affirmatively, you are predestined to be saved. If you are lost, it will be because you chose to be. Note why some are lost: "Because when I called, ye did not answer; when I spake, ye did not hear; but did evil before mine eyes, and did choose that wherein I delighted not" (Isaiah 65:12).

There is only one thing that can separate you from Jesus, and that is your own choice. No wonder Paul says: "If God is for us, who can be against us? He who did not spare his own Son, but gave him up for us all—how will he not also, along with him, graciously give us all things? . . . Who shall separate us from the love of Christ? Shall trouble or hardship or persecution or famine or nakedness or danger or sword? . . . No, in all these things we are more than conquerors through him who loved us. For I am convinced that neither death nor life, neither angels nor demons, neither the present nor the future, nor any powers, neither height nor depth, nor anything else in all creation, will be able to separate us from the love of God that is in Christ Jesus our Lord" (Romans 8:31-39, NIV). "Being confident of this very thing, that he which hath begun a good work in you will perform it until the day of Jesus Christ" (Philippians 1:6). "Lay hold upon the hope set before us: which hope we have as an anchor of the soul, both sure and steadfast" (Hebrews 6:19).

Now you have a right to say, "Pastor, you have been saying that we can be sure of life eternal. Are you sure? Do you think you 'have it made' and that you are 'in'? How does it feel?"

If you ask me that question, I must answer it this way: When you meet me in the kingdom of heaven, and you ask me how I got there, do you think I will say, "Well, I tell you, I worked hard; I denied myself all the pleasures of the world of sin; I struggled in my warfare with the forces of evil until I finally made it"? And if I should answer thus, do you think the angels in heaven will strike up the chorus: "Worthy is the Lamb that was slain to receive power, and riches, and wisdom, and strength, and honour, and glory, and blessing"? In no way.

When you meet me in the kingdom and ask, "Elder Heubach, how did you get here?" I will answer, "It is only by the grace of God that I am here. He was so kind, so gracious, and so long-suffering. He put up with my littleness, my selfishness, my pride, and all my weaknesses—well, friend, it is only because of His goodness and His love that I am here." And do you know what you will say? You will say the same.

Can I be sure of life eternal? Yes. Because I am so good? No, because He is. Then the angels will strike up the wonderful anthem of praise.

Chapter 15

Is It Worth It?

"Look, we have left everything and followed you. What is that going to be worth to us?" (Matthew 19:27, Phillips).

For the kingdom of Heaven is like a farmer going out early in the morning to hire laborers for his vineyard. He agreed with them on a wage of a silver coin a day and sent them to work. About nine o'clock he went out and saw some others standing about in the market place with nothing to do. "You go to the vineyard too," he said to them, "and I will pay you a fair wage." And off they went. At about midday and again at about three o'clock in the afternoon he went out and said the same thing. Then about five o'clock he went out and found some others standing about. "Why are you standing about here all day doing nothing?" he asked them. "Because no one has employed us," they replied. "You go off into the vineyard as well, then," he said.

When evening came the owner of the vineyard said to his foreman, "Call the laborers and pay them their wages, beginning with the last and ending with the first." So those who were engaged at five o'clock came up and each man received a silver coin. But when the first to be employed came they reckoned they would get more, but they also received a silver coin a man. As they took their money they grumbled at the farmer and said, "These last fellows have only put in one hour's work and you've treated them exactly the same as us who have gone through all the hard work and heat of the day!"

But he replied to one of them: "My friend, I'm not being unjust to you. Wasn't our agreement for a silver coin a day? Take your money and go home. It is my wish to give the latecomer as much as I give you. May I not do what I like with what belongs to me? Must you be jealous because I am generous?"

So, many who are the last now will be first then and the first last (Matthew 20:1-16, Phillips).

"He went away sad, because he had great wealth" (Matthew 19:22, NIV). That is the record of an outstanding young man, who should have been a happy man from all outward appearances. He was a moral man, successful, secure, and wealthy; but something was lacking inside. He had come to Jesus to talk about it. He said, " 'What is still missing in my life?' " (verse 20, Phillips).

Jesus loved that young man. He wanted to help him. So He said to him, " 'If you want to be perfect, go now and sell your property and give the money away to the poor—you will have riches in Heaven. Then come and follow me!' " (verse 21, Phillips). It was then that he went away sad.

Instead of seeing in Jesus' answer that which would satisfy what was missing in his life, he saw only what he had to give up. So many of us are like that. We see only the things we have to give up or sacrifice for Jesus and miss altogether what He really offers. The young man didn't realize that the greatness of a sacrifice is not measured in terms of what is given *up*, but what is given *to*. If the young man had given up everything, that in itself would not have satisfied his lack. He missed the last part of Jesus' answer, "Come and follow me."

Jesus never asks us to give up anything except for

something better. He didn't ask every rich man to give away his wealth. Many became great supporters of His cause. He only asked this young man to give up what he was doing in order to give him something far more creative and rewarding to do. This would have satisfied what was lacking inside. Jesus had great plans for this rich young ruler. It was the same kind of call He gave the twelve disciples.

In the parable of the pearl of great price, the man sold everything he had. But that was not what was commendable; it was his buying the Precious Pearl. A meaningful sacrifice is one that gives up something for something more important, like a sacrifice hit in a baseball game.

The rich young executive went away sad. He didn't think it was worth it. As he went, Jesus, too, was sad. There follows a discussion that really shook the disciples on how hard it is for rich men to get into the kingdom of heaven. Their response was, " 'Who then can be saved?' "

Finally Peter said, " 'Look, we have left everything and followed you. What is that going to be worth to us?' " (verse 27, Phillips).

Jesus didn't rebuke Peter for asking this question. He could have. He could have said, "Peter, I'm surprised at you. If you are interested only in what you are going to get out of it, you are not fit to be My disciple." But He didn't say that. He presented a threefold reward that thrilled the hearts of those who heard Him. And it was then that Jesus told the story of the laborers quoted at the beginning of this chapter.

What is Jesus saying in this parable?

What do you think would be the reaction today if those who did a little work just for an hour before quitting time received the same pay as those who had worked hard all day? I am sure the employer would have real problems on his hands the next day if he continued to follow this practice. Who would be so stupid as to go to work at six in the morning, if he could get a full paycheck by coming to work at five o'clock in the evening?

Surely the right proportioning of wages is justified in business, isn't it? A man should be properly compensated for his work, but a part-time worker cannot be paid as much as the full-time man on the job. Nor can even the janitor be paid the same as the vice-president of a great corporation. But two men who do the same job and have the same training should receive at least approximately the same wages.

To understand what Jesus meant by the parable we need to remember that it was part of His answer to Peter's statement: " 'We have left everything and followed you. What is that going to be worth to us?' " If this is true, the men could have said, "Lord, we have given up our jobs, we have sacrificed a great deal to follow You. Are we going to get no more in the end than those who take it easy and enjoy life until they grow too old and worn out to do anything else and then suddenly have an attack of religion? You mean to say that those who delay conversion until the last hour and then sneak in under the wire will fare as well as we?"

And apparently Jesus' answer is, "That is right. Anyone who comes even at the last hour will be paid by me in full."

Isn't that rather hard to understand? If this is true, what should keep us from postponing our acceptance of Jesus' invitation until a more convenient season? One might say, "Well, you might be killed suddenly and not have a chance." Right, but is the motive of fear the right motive for serving Jesus? That doesn't sound right.

Take for example the prodigal son. He wasted his substance in riotous living. When he returned to his father's house a great feast was prepared to welcome him. You can just imagine the elder brother saying to himself, "If I had known this, I would have gone with my brother when he left."

What is Jesus saying to us in this parable?

He is saying first of all that entrance into the kingdom of heaven is not based on a merit system—"not of works, lest any man should boast" (Ephesians 2:9). He is saying that in service for God the rewards are not something earned or merited but something experienced. Why is the kingdom of heaven not a merit system? Because love is not such.

You do not earn or merit love by brownie points. "My Christmas gift for you cost me twenty-five dollars. You only spent five dollars on mine. I had to work a whole week to save enough money to buy your present. You only had to work one day. You don't love me as much as I love you." What would you think of this kind of love relationship?

When you understand the nature of the kingdom of heaven you see things in a different perspective. You see that the privilege of working in Christ's vineyard is itself a reward, a great joy, an undreamed-of fulfillment. There is a song we used to sing in Sabbath School that goes like this, "O there'll be joy when the work is done." Jesus is saying that when you really understand His work, you will sing, "Oh, there is joy in doing the work." In some respects, is not a job to do better than a job done? There is real satisfaction in having completed something worthwhile—a job well done—but if that should be the end with no more to do, the joy would not last. To be doing something creative that you can do well, that you greatly enjoy doing, that is worthwhile, brings real happiness and satisfaction to a person's life. The joy of service in service is part of the reward of working for Christ. As glorious as the end of a journey may be, there are times when experiences along the way are just as exciting.

On one occasion an academy senior startled his classmates with a statement, "I'm not sure I want to go to heaven." He was a lad interested in electronics and aviation, and he somehow felt that these things might not be needed in the earth made new. A fellow student pointed out that to him it would be exciting to just think about being at a place and find himself there. To which our senior replied: "That is just the trouble. It's not getting somewhere that interests me as much as manipulating the gadgets along the way."

Engaging in interesting, meaningful, creative activity is very rewarding in itself. This is what the service of Jesus offers. The rewards of serving Christ, you see, begin immediately upon your decision to serve Him. They are not saved until the end of the day. And the glory of it all is that this joy will continue throughout all eternity. The future reward will be the privilege of having always something new to do and to enjoy.

"Just think," says the veteran, "I had the joy of serving for fifty years in the cause of God. Oh, yes, there were times when my bones ached and the sweat blinded my eyes and it seemed I could not go on. But I don't regret a moment of it. Peace after pain is a joy not even angels know."

The idea will never occur to the latecomers—if they really understand who He is that has called them and catch a glimpse of the love of God in true perspective—to laugh at the others because they worked through the heat of the day while they themselves "got off easy." They will not say, "Thank God that we got our reward so cheaply." Or "Thank goodness a last-minute repentance is enough." Rather they will say with Johannes Scheffler:

> Alas, that I so lately knew Thee;
> Thee, so worthy of the best;
> Nor had sooner turned to view Thee,
> Truest good and only rest!
> The more I love,
> I mourn the more
> That I did not love before!

You see what I mean when I say, "In service for God the rewards are not something earned or merited but something experienced."

Let us look, however, at Jesus' answer to Peter concerning the future for the Christian (see Matthew 19:28, 29).

First, "When the Son of Man sits on his glorious throne, you who have followed me will also sit on twelve thrones"(NIV). In other words, you will share with Christ in enterprises of responsible, creative activity.

Second, "You will receive a hundredfold." In other words, you will receive a 10,000 percent increase, or dividends, on your investment. What you have given up will sink into insignificance in comparison with what you will receive.

Third, "You will inherit eternal life." In other words, for you there will be never-ending joy. You will receive not simply some gift for past exploits, but you will enjoy opportunities for further service under conditions you cannot now fully comprehend. Throughout eternity all of life's greatest values will be experienced and appreciated with ever-increasing satisfaction.

"There the redeemed shall know, even as also they are known. The loves and sympathies which God Himself has planted in the soul shall there find truest and sweetest exercise. . . .

"There the grandest enterprises may be carried forward, the loftiest aspirations reached, the highest ambitions realized; and still there will arise new heights to surmount, new wonders to admire, new truths to comprehend, fresh objects to call forth the powers of mind and soul and body" (*The Great Controversy*, p. 677).

Picture with me in your imagination the glorious scene of the coronation of the Son of God after the millennium. The great motion picture in which are reviewed the facts of the great controversy for all to see has just finished. Jesus has just been crowned King of kings and Lord of lords. "He looks upon the redeemed, renewed in His own image, every heart bearing the perfect impress of the divine, every face reflecting the likeness of their King. He beholds in them the result of the travail of His soul, and He is satisfied. Then, in a voice that reaches the assembled multitudes of the righteous and the wicked, He declares: 'Behold the purchase of My blood! For these I suffered, for these I died, that they might dwell in My presence throughout eternal ages.' And the song of praise ascends from the white-robed ones about the throne: 'Worthy is the Lamb that was slain to receive power, and riches, and wisdom, and strength, and honor, and glory, and blessing' " (*ibid.*, p. 671).

Just imagine what it will be to join in that oratorio

of praise. That alone would be worth it all. But to look up into the face of Jesus and see there that smile of satisfaction on His countenance and to realize that we had a part in bringing Him that joy will be the greatest reward.

Then perhaps, when there comes a pause in the music, someone by your side will nudge you and say, "You know, friend, if it weren't for you, I wouldn't be here today. When I was just about ready to give up, you encouraged me. When I thought all was lost, you led me to Him. Oh, man, thanks a million!" That will be joy unspeakable for both, won't it?

Too often we think only of what Jesus can do for us. This is wonderful, but to think of what we can do for Him is even more rewarding. Throughout eternity we shall continue to sing His praises and to declare to all we meet the wonders of His love and the glorious character of our God.

Is it worth it?

What do you think?

The Donkey-Cart Kids

Bobbie Montgomery

Father is dead and Mother is in a sanitarium to recover her health, and the five Larkin children stare in horror as their pet goat swallows the last bits of their train tickets to Grandma's house. Alone in the midst of tragedy, they hitch up the family donkey and set out on their own, beginning an adventure you won't soon forget. Available September, 1980. Paper.

FLEE THE CAPTOR

Herbert Ford

The gripping story of John Henry Weidner, hero of history's greatest holocaust. As a member of the Dutch-Paris Underground, Weidner helped save the lives of over nine hundred Jews and Allied pilots trying to escape the terror of Nazism. Paper.

PROJECT Sunlight

JUNE STRONG

The story of an upstate New York woman as told by her guardian angel and how she learns of God's love for her and experiences his protection in the closing weeks before Christ's return. A thought-provoking story to be enjoyed by Christians of any denomination. Coming September, 1980. Paper.

THE RISE & FALL OF SUPER WOMAN

Carole Sheron

She had to achieve more, do more, be everything to everybody, for she feared losing the love and respect of her family, friends—and even God. So she turned to drugs and found she could add an extra day to her week. But it almost killed her. A personal story of how one woman found in a loving, accepting God the courage to accept her human limitations. Paper.

TAMING YOUR TV AND OTHER MEDIA

David Schwantes

This Christian consumer's guide to the modern mass media teaches how to escape the trap of "teleholism," what can be done about the rising flood of pornography, and how to use the media wisely in your home. Paper.

Teetering on the Tightrope

Carol Amen

Practical pointers are given on how to balance all the pressures and responsibilities that keep both men and women walking an emotional tightrope. Paper.

TRIAL BY DEATH AND FIRE

D. Carl Anderson

The author had waited a long time to start a ranch for homeless boys. One night an inner voice said, "Do it now." From that moment began an amazing tale of modern faith. Despite lack of money, hostility, prejudice, arson, death, and enough other problems to break most men, he pursued his dream to success. A true story of faith in God that you won't be able to put down. Available in September, 1980. Paper.

Unblessed

Berneice Lunday

Religious persecution is not a thing of the past, as Margaret finds out when she decides to marry outside her faith. A story of the cruelty of prejudice in one woman's search for happiness and a religious faith that included a loving God. An unforgettable account of courage and love. Paper.

UNLEASHED

Leon Orr

The bestselling story of Duane and Laurel, their trials and heartaches, as their love for each other grows in the last few months before Christ's second coming. Paper.

Where Are We Running?

June Strong

Her typically uncommon way of looking at common occurrences has endeared June Strong to thousands of readers through her monthly column in *These Times* magazine. These qualities, along with her commonsense wit and wisdom, express themselves beautifully in several favorite selections from *These Times*, gathered into this captivating volume. Paper.